I0422536

Short Plays on Reproductive Freedom

34 Short Plays and Performance Pieces from the Reproductive Freedom Festival and Words of Choice

Curated by **Cindy Cooper**
with **Stacey Linnartz**, artistic coordinator

Original works by creative writers on reproductive freedom, health, rights and justice for reading or performance

This collection is published by
Words of Choice, Inc.
New York City
Copyright 2018
All Rights Reserved

Ebook edition 2018: 978-1-912924-02-8
Print edition 2019: 978-1-078109-41-3

For information or details:
Cindy Cooper, Words of Choice
reproductivefreedomfestival@gmail.com
wordsofchoice@mindspring.com

Cover Art by Jessica Noele DeWitt

Published by: Words of Choice, Inc.

SHORT PLAYS ON REPRODUCTIVE FREEDOM
From the Reproductive Freedom Festival and Words of Choice, Inc.

Introduction
Short Plays on Reproductive Freedom offers 34 short plays or performance works that recognize and celebrate the fundamental human right to bodily autonomy. This rich collection of works, each approximately five minutes long, explores reproductive rights, health, freedom and justice, aiming to generate new conversations about these important topics.

A Collection of Works
We invite you to be taken away by these writings.
The pieces in this collection are meant to spark the imagination and stir the soul, as good theater can do. They are rewarding reading, alone or in a group. All have been performed live. Each was included in the Reproductive Freedom Festival, a live and live streaming festival of new works about reproductive rights, health, freedom and justice in 2016. This publication is an acknowledgement of their continuing relevance: these topics remain vital to society and the search for social justice.

The Writers
The writers include: **Grisel Acosta, Judith Arcana, Marcy Arlin, Melissa Bell, Angela Bonavoglia, Stephen Cedars, Kitty Chen, Ellen Cohen, Cindy Cooper, Allie Costa, Marjorie Duffield, Jessica Feder-Birnbaum, Anne Flanagan, Nicole Goodwin, Yvette Heyliger, Home|Work Collective, Henry Howard, Michael angel Johnson, Mildred Lewis, Samantha Lierens, Jessica Litwak, Zoneziwoh Mbondgulo-Wondieh, Junita Middleton, Debbie Miller, Winter Miller, Alix Olson, Marge Piercy, Jeremy Rishe, Mercedes Sanchez, Laura A. Shamas, Laura Zlatos.**

The Short Plays

The short plays and performance pieces are divided into six general sections: **Heroines; Next Generations; Conflicts; Body Politics; Discoveries**; and **What We Know.** In addition, **three special sections** add to the selections – **Ireland 2016, Song Lyrics**, and **Additional Writings**. The selections include monologues and dialogue-driven work, spoken word, performable essays, poems and lyrics, both comedic and dramatic. The plays or other selections may be performed individually or in groups tailored by the performer. (Please note that individual writer permission is required for use of any selection.)

Topics of the Plays

The plays in this collection cover a wide range of topics, as is fitting to the many concerns that fall under the umbrella of Reproductive Freedom. The topics include: pregnancy, abortion, contraception, birthing, adoption, parenthood, nonparenthood, healthcare, politics, incarceration, cancer, aging, rape, racism, antiabortion harassment, medical care, activism, leadership, stigma, history, community, bodily autonomy, friendship, individuality, absurdity, real and imagined futures, and storytelling of all sorts and types.

Use of Plays

The plays and selections in this volume may only be performed with specific permission of the writer. **Contact the writer** directly (see the section WRITERS below for biographical information about the writers) or reach out to reproductivefreedomfestival@gmail.com with the subject heading 'Permission.'

What to know about Reproductive Freedom

Reproductive freedom touches upon topics related to reproductive healthcare, sex, sexuality, birthing, parenting, gender roles, abortion, contraception, and more, as well as activism and the drive toward recognition of equality for all. Reproductive freedom is an expression of the universal values of bodily autonomy and self-determination. It represents the individual's right to be free from government intrusion, as well as from outside force, danger or judgment on matters of reproductive decision-making.

At a time where our reproductive freedoms are being challenged and stigmatized, these selections raise the voices of talented theater artists and other writers and open new doors to the important role of culture in bringing vibrant stories to the public about human rights and social justice.

More Information
The Reproductive Freedom Festival was produced by *Words of Choice, Inc.* and curated by **Cindy Cooper** with **Stacey Linnartz** serving as artistic consultant and coordinator. It was performed in New York City and live streamed by producing partner **VirtualArts TV, Kathryn Velvel Jones**, executive director, to all fifty states and 10 countries.

Visit the **Reproductive Freedom Festival** website, **www.reproductivefreedomfestival.org** for additional information, or the publisher, **Words of Choice, Inc.**, www.wordsofchoice.org.

Contact Us:
reproductivefreedomfestival@gmail.com

WRITERS (alphabetically by last name followed by their selection in this volume in italics)

Dr. Grisel Y. Acosta (*Hardcore Latina Punk Birth Fragments* in Section One) is a writer from Chicago and is currently an assistant professor at Bronx Community College—City University of New York. Her creative work is in *Nineteen Sixty Nine: An Ethnic Studies Journal, MiPoesias, Pembroke Magazine, Private International Photo Review*, the NAACP Image Award nominated *Check the Rhyme, Chicago's After Hours Magazine, Love You Madly*, and the forthcoming *Basta!: 100 Latinas Write on Violence Against Women.*

Judith Arcana (*In the Service we said* and *Women's Liberation*, both in Section Two) is a writer and a Jane, a member of Chicago's pre-Roe underground abortion service. She's written about abortion and other motherhood themes for many years – read *What if your mother* (poetry collection); *Keesha and Joanie and JANE* (fiction zine); and *Soon To Be A Major Motion Picture* (fiction chapbook) + more stories, poems and essays in journals, anthologies and newspapers. See juditharcana.com for links.

Marcy Arlin (*Lucky Old Lady* in Section One) is Artistic Director of the OBIE-winning Immigrants' Theatre Project, directing/producing over 200 plays. Member: Brooklyn Speculative Fiction Writers, Broad Universe, Theatre Without Borders, No Passport, LPTW, Lincoln Center Directors Lab. She studied fiction with award-winning authors Chris McKitterick, Andy Duncan, Kij Johnson, Betsy James, Jill Dearman. Published science fiction in *Daily Science Fiction, PerihelionSF.com, others,* as well as articles in *Czech Plays: 7 New Works* (editor) and TCGcircle. Marcy has taught theatre at Yale, Brown, CUNY, U. of Chicago (her alma mater), and Pace. She is a Fulbright scholar to Romania and the Czech Republic.

Melissa Bell (*Playground Placenta* in Section One) is the writer of plays and librettos that have been presented at the Triad, Snapple Theatre, TheatreLab, and the Bechdel

Group's 24-hour challenge. <u>Librettos:</u> Off-Broadway: *Devil & The Deep*, Reimagining Treasure Island. Music/Lyrics: Graham Russell (Air Supply) & Katie McGhie, Theatre East. *Lost In Love*, Triad Theater, featuring Constantine Maroulis and Andrea McArdle. Plays: *Love, Sex, Anarchy*, Corner Store Arts Center, excerpts at National Museum of Women in the Arts, Washington DC. 29th Street Playwrights Collective Member.

Angela Bonavoglia (*Women and ...?* by Angela Bonavoglia in Section Two) is the author of the nonfiction book, *Good Catholic Girls: How Women Are Leading the Fight to Change the Church*, and the classic oral history, *The Choices We Made: 25 Women and Men Speak Out About Abortion*. She has also written for *Ms.* (former contributing editor), the *Chicago Tribune*, *The Nation*, *Salon*, *Rewire*, *Religion Dispatches*, Women's Media Center, and the Huffington Post, and other publications.

Stephen Cedars (*Certain Doom* in Section Three) is an award-winning writer, director and teacher originally from south Louisiana. In addition to producing or creating work throughout New York City, he has had plays published and produced throughout the country. Among his awards are the Theater Masters Visionary Playwright Award, a Fellowship with Target Margin, a Residency with America-in-Play, and the John Golden Playwriting Prize. He earned his MFA in Dramatic Writing from NYU, which he attended as a Rita and Burton Goldberg Fellow.

Kitty Chen (*A Change of Heart, So to Speak* in Section Five) is an autodidact and a multiple award-winning playwright (NEA, 2 NYFAs, among others). She has been working in the theater since 1975, first as a modern dancer, now as actor and playwright. Born in Shanghai, China, and raised near Philadelphia, she got a BA in math from Brown and fled science and academia for New York and a life in the arts.

Ellen Cohen (*The Prisoner* in Section Four), Midwife, delivered 1,400 babies in New York City hospitals as well as provided contraceptive care to her patients, who included low-paid workers, immigrants, teenagers and women with mental or physical disabilities. She participated in research that led to the first breakthrough in preventing mother-to-child transmission of HIV. She authored *Laboring: Stories of a New York City Hospital Midwife*, from which her piece in this show is adapted.

Cindy Cooper (*Rhymes with Ryan (On the Hill 2016)* in Section Three, and *Tru Luv* in Section Nine) is an award-winning playwright and journalist. Her play, *How She Played the Game*, was performed off-Broadway at The Women's Project and later at Primary Stages, and has been performed in 100 other venues. *Strange Light* was produced at Wings in NY, Bailiwick in Chicago, Philadelphia and Buffalo. *Silence Not, A Love Story* premiered in Jerusalem and a published version won a prize for historic fiction. Her plays are published in 15 volumes. She is the founder and producer of Words of Choice, which mounted the Reproductive Freedom Festival and has toured a theater performance in support of reproductive freedom and rights for 15 years, winning awards from NARAL Pro-Choice America and the Abortion Conversation Project. She is a two-time Jerome Fellow and lives in New York City.

Allie Costa (*Two Girls* in Section Two) works in film, TV, theatre, and voiceover as an actor, screenwriter, playwright, director, and singer. Her acting credits include *Spring Awakening, 90210, Hamlet,* and *You Me & Her.* Her plays have been produced internationally, including *Femme Noir, How I Knew Her, A Taste of the Future,* and *Can You Keep a Secret?* A gender-neutral version of *Two Girls* entitled TWO is also available for performance and licensing; please contact Allie directly for more information.allie@alliecosta.com http://www.alliecosta.com

Marjorie Duffield (*Not So Fresh Feeling* and *These Breasts Can Kill,* both in Section Eight*)* is a playwright and librettist. Theater: *Ice Island: The Wait For Shackelton* (off-Broadway); *Sit-In at the Five & Dime,* music by Janice Lowe (New

Harmony Project, Voice & Vision, Dixon Place); *In A Lake Of Fire*, music by Greg Pliska (Winner, Moss Hart Award and Finalist, Richard Rodgers Awards); *Cyber-Alice*, music by Sunmee Cho (Lincoln Center Directors Lab at HERE). She is a recipient of the Jonathan Larson Memorial Musical Theatre Fellowship. The selections here are from TIT-Tales, a body politics cabaret with music by **Greg Pliska** who has also composed for *Sylvia* (Broadway); *Comedy of Errors, As You Like It* (co-composer with Steve Martin), *Twelfth Night* (arranger) and more. TIT-TALEs premiered at the WOW Café Theater in New York City in 1996 and was later produced at Williams College; songs and selections have been included in many social justice events.

Jessica Feder-Birnbaum (*Mid Life Choice* in Section Five) has written for stage and screen. A reading of her musical, *Margaret Sanger - A Woman Rebel,* was held at the Richmond Shepard Theatre. She directs multi-generational theatre pieces. Her articles and prose pieces have appeared in print and on-line. She is an MFTA Summer Institute scholarship recipient (New York State Council on the Arts).

Anne Flanagan (*Useless Uterus* in Section Four) is a writer/actor/teacher/and entrepreneur. She's also worked as a private investigator, which was not nearly as exciting as one might think. Her plays have been produced throughout the US and internationally. Publications include *Artifice* (Dramatic Publishing), *Best Women's Monologues 2013* (Smith and Kraus) and *Best Contemporary Monologues 2014*(Applause) among others. Anne is the recipient of several writing awards and absolutely no sports trophies. Website: http://anneflanagan.net

Nicole Goodwin (*Ain't I A Woman* in Section Six) is the *2013-2014 Queer Art Mentorship* Queer Art Literary Fellow, as well as the winner of The Fresh Fruit Festival's 2013 Award for Performance Poetry. She is also the finalist for the *Poet House* 2013 Poet House Emerging Poets Fellowship Program. Recently, she published the articles "Talking with My Daughter..." and "Why is this Happening in Your Life..." (Personal essay/Review for award-winning documentary

Tough Love) in the *New York Times'* parentblog *Motherlode*. Additionally, her work "Desert Flowers" was shortlisted and selected for performance by the Women Playwriting International Conference this summer in Cape Town, South Africa.

Yvette Heyliger (*On The Brink of Middle Age* in Section Four) is an award-winning playwright, a director and a producing artist. She is the recipient of the AUDELCO Recognition Award for Excellence in Black Theatre's August Wilson Playwright Award and a Best Playwright nomination from the NAACP's Annual Theatre Awards, to name a few. A partner in Twinbiz™, she is the co-recipient of the first National Black Theatre Festival Emerging Producer Award. After many years on the other side of the footlights, Yvette returned to the stage in her first one-woman show, *Bridge to Baraka*. Yvette's plays have been published on line by indietheaternow.com and stagereads.com. She is a contributing author to two collections of plays, *24 Gun Control Plays* and *WE ARE THEATRE*, as well as a collection of poetry, *No Limits*. Her work was selected for *Best Women's Stage Monologues 2003* and *Best Stage Scenes 2003*. Yvette has written articles and blogs for *The Dramatist, Black Masks, Continuum,* and *HowlRound*. The author of *Autobiography of a Homegirl*, she will soon release a collection of plays, *What a Piece of Work is Man! Full-Length Plays for Leading Women*. Yvette is a proud member of the Dramatist Guild, AEA, SDC, and SAG-AFTRA. http://www.twinbiz.com/yvette_res.html

The home|work Collective (*The Renunciation* in Section Seven) and *The Renunciation*, included in the Reproductive Freedom Festival, emerged from research and development undertaken by artist Siobhán Clancy (www.siobhanclancy.com) with activist members of the Abortion Rights Campaign in Ireland (www.abortionrights.ie). It was funded under The Arts Council Artist in the Community Scheme managed by Create (The National Development Agency for Collaborative Arts) in Ireland with mentorship by performance artist Áine Phillips. Special thanks to A4 Sounds Studio, Dublin, Ireland. *The Renunciation* has been performed in Bangkok, Belfast, Berlin, Cork, Dublin, Galway, London, Limerick, Maynooth and New York. **www.home-workcollective.tumblr.com**

Henry Howard (*The Last Refuge* in Section Five) is a Los Angeles poet and fiction writer, who works in the genre of human rights literature. He writes: "The struggle for full, unrestricted reproductive rights is deeply personal to me, and I have been a national and local clinic defender since 1988. Forced motherhood is female enslavement, and if half the world is not free, none of us are free! Abortion on demand, and without apology." *(Editor's note: d. April 23, 2019.)*

Michael angel Johnson (*The Goddess of Hygieia* in Section Four) Michael angel Johnson's *The Price of Solitude* was a finalist in the National Ten-Minute Play Contest at Actors Theatre of Louisville. *The Apartment* earned her the honor of special participant at the O'Neill Theatre Center. The author of "The African American Woman Who Shaped the Future of Art" *(On The Issues Magazine)*, Michael angel is a member of The League of Professional Theatre Women and New York Women in Film & Television. She is a graduate of The Yale School of Drama.

Mildred Lewis (*Chained Labor* in Section Four) After Oberlin College, Mildred began as a director at the Actors Studio and Circle Repertory's LAB. After graduating from UCLA's film school, she won Samuel Goldwyn and HBO New Writers Awards. *Unbowed,* a feature based on her work, screened at the Palm Springs, American Indian and Pan African Film Festivals. Her plays have been produced in Chicago, Cincinnati, London, New York and Spokane. She teaches English at Chapman University and has won several teaching awards.

Samantha Lierens *(Savita* in Section Seven) is from London, UK. She writes: "I'm a new playwright and I'm passionate about women's rights so it's been wonderful to combine these two loves for the Reproductive Freedom Festival. I have an MA in creative writing and a degree in politics. I've published four erotic books under a pseudonym and I am currently working on a young adult romance novel and a stage play about the 1970 protests against Miss World. The story of 'Savita,' presented in the Reproductive Freedom Festival, still shocks me in that a young woman could be so comprehensibly failed by the system."

Jessica Litwak, Ph.D. *(Terrible Virtue* in Section One) is a theatre artist focused on theatre for social change. She is a playwright, actor, educator, drama therapist and the Director of The H.E.A.T. Collective. She is a Fulbright Specialist Scholar. Her work has been published by No Passport Press, TCG, Applause Books, Smith and Kraus, *The New York Times*, and produced Off-Broadway and on international stages. As an actress, she's appeared in film, television and theatres across the U.S. Her play in the Reproductive Freedom Festival, *Terrible Virtue,* was originally developed at The Lark Theatre with director Daniella Topol. Litwak did undercover research in the field with Americans United For Life and Operation Rescue, as well as working closely with NARAL and the Center for Reproductive Rights.

Zoneziwoh Mbondgulo-Wondieh (@ZoFem) (*Why I March* in Section Nine) is an award-winning humanitarian feminist storyteller, executive director of Women for a Change, Cameroon (@Wfaccmr). She holds a Masters in Sex, Gender, and Violence, and has over ten years of experience working, researching, documenting, and advocating for the promoting of women's human rights, leadership, and development in and out of Africa. You can learn more about Zoneziwoh's works and feminist activism through the different social media links: Twitter / Instagram / Tumblr: @ZoFem/Facebook: Zoneziwoh Mbondgulo-Wondieh/LinkedIn / Google + : Zoneziwoh/ Blog: zofem.blogspot.com

Junita Middleton (*American Girl/Igbo World* in Section Three) was born and raised in Brooklyn, New York. She is a graduate of Lincoln University where she obtained her B.S. in Health Science. Junita had intentions to become

13

a Physical Therapist, but over the years she returned to her true passion - writing. She now aspires to become a television writer and director. Currently, Junita is writing and directing a documentary about her late great-grandmother.

Debbie L. Miller (*Ida Mae Murphy* in Section Six) writes plays, monologues, short stories, humor, memoir, and essays. Her monologue "Ida Mae Murphy" is part of a series that includes a one-person show (*Driving to Hawaii*), a play (*Caravan Women*), a short story (*Bonnie's Journey*), a screenplay (*Mushers*), and four monologues. Miller's plays have been produced in and outside of NYC. She wears many hats including freelance journalist and actor. She lives in Brooklyn.

Winter Miller (*Spare Rib – excerpts from a play* in Section Six) was raised by feminist activists in New England hamlets from which she emerged relatively similar to the adorable wolves who raised her. Founding member of the Obie-winning 13Playwrights. Winter digs provocative, honest people. Like bells and whistles? Visit www.wintermiller.com

Alix Olson (*blessed – excerpts* in Section Six) is an internationally touring spoken word artist-activist. http://www.alixolson.com/

Marge Piercy (*Heroines* in Section One) Knopf recently published Marge Piercy's 19th poetry book *Made in Detroit* as well *The Hunger Moon: New & Selected Poems* in paperback. Piercy wrote 17 novels , most recently *Sex Wars*; PM Press republished *Dance The Eagle To Sleep*, *Vida* and *Braided Lives* with new introductions, her first short story collection, *The Cost of Lunch, Etc.* and, recently, *My Life, My Body*, essays, interview and poems. Her memoir is *Sleeping With Cats*, Harper Perennial. www.margepiercy.com

Jeremy Rishe (*Cobra This!* in Section Three) writes, acts and directs with Third Wing Media. He's a founding board member of Kids Creative Collective, which brings theater to young people in NYC. Select acting credits: TV/Film: *Hard Candy Kid, The Black Box, Elementary, The Good Wife, Law & Order: SVU, Blue Bloods, The Weekend* (co-writing credit), *Two Night Stand.* Select Off-Broadway: *The Megile of Itzik Manger, Sex On Sunday, Starry Messenger, Jewtopia*; Regional: Ala Shakes, Cleveland Playhouse, Pioneer Theatre, elsewhere. He holds an MFA from NYU's Graduate Acting Program.

Mercedes Sanchez (*Sister* in Section Six) is honored to be included in the Reproductive Freedom Festival and this anthology. They combine two of her passions, reproductive rights and writing. By day, Mercedes works at Cedar River Clinics, a proud abortion provider in Washington State. By night, Mercedes writes plays, poetry, and short stories. She would like to dedicate her monologue, Sister, to all abortion providers, and especially to the amazing staff of Cedar River Clinics, for their compassion and courage.

Laura Shamas (*Papyrus* in Section Five) has written forty plays. Writing projects include her new full-length play *Merrion Square*, and completing a novel (knock wood, fingers crossed, etc.). She is a co-founder, with Jennie Webb, of the Los Angeles Female Playwrights Initiative (lafpi.com). Her play *Circular* was on The Kilroys 2015 List (Honorable Mention). Website: laurashamas.com.

Laura Zlatos (*The Pill* in Section Two) is a Brooklyn-based theater artist and resident playwright with the Exquisite Corpse Company. Recent playwriting credits include: *Happily After Ever* (59E59 Theaters, Edinburgh Fringe Festival, Signature Theatre), *Exposure* (Gene Frankel Theater) *Secession 2015* (New Orleans Faux/Real Festival of the Arts, Governers Island), *The Weird Tree* (New York International Fringe Festival), *Things I Never Learned in Physics* (Rattlestick Playwrights Theater), and *Three Hours* (HERE Arts Center). Laura is a recipient of the 2016 Woodward/Newman Drama Award (*Happily After Ever*) and a winner of the 2012 Chameleon Theatre Circle's New Play Contest (*The Light in the Refrigerator*). She has been a finalist for the Jerome Fellowship, the Princess Grace Playwriting Fellowship, the MFA Playwrights' Workshop at the Kennedy Center, and the Reva Shiner Comedy Award. She received her MFA in Playwriting from Columbia University, her MA in Performance Studies from NYU, and her BFA in Dramatic Writing and Gender and Sexuality Studies from NYU. www.laurazlatos.com

Directors in the Reproductive Freedom Festival (alphabetically by last name)

Francesca Mantani Arkus, (director, **Section Three – CONFLICTS**) has worked at the Hudson Guild, Anne Frank Center, HERE, Signature, Blue Heron, Phil Bosakowski Theatre, 78th Street, The Director's Company, Barrow Group, Pulse Ensemble, with Words of Choice, and in readings at New York Theatre Workshop and the Public Theatre. Regionally, she's worked at Mark Taper Forum, Capitol Theatre and the Open Eye. She served as Assistant Director to Tina Landau on *Floyd Collins* at Playwrights Horizons, and is a director/dramaturg with NYU's Tisch School of the Arts.

Marcy Arlin (director, **Section Five – DISCOVERIES**, with directing by **Muriel Miguel**) is Artistic Director of the OBIE-winning Immigrants' Theatre Project, directing/producing over 200 plays. Member: Brooklyn Speculative Fiction Writers, Broad Universe, Theatre Without Borders, No Passport, LPTW, Lincoln Center Directors Lab. Marcy has taught theatre at Yale, Brown, CUNY, U. of Chicago (her alma mater), and Pace. She is a Fulbright scholar to Romania and the Czech Republic. **Muriel Miguel** is a founding member and artistic director of Spiderwoman Theater, where she has worked as a director, choreographer, playwright, actor and educator.

Thais Flaitt Giannoccaro, (director, **Special Section – IRELAND PRE SHOW**) worked in Brazil as an actress, producer and teaching artist. In the U.S. since 2007, she has directed the world premieres of Kim Kershner's *All in*

the Mind, Caridad Svich's *The Archaeology of Dreams*, and Erlina Ortiz's *Morir Sonyando*, among others. She is in the first theatre cohort of Lincoln Center Scholars, teaching in two public schools. She has an MA in Theatre from the University of Nebraska at Omaha and a BA in Art Education from the University of Belas Artes of Sao Paolo (Brazil).

Joan Kane (director, **Section One, HEROINES)** is the founding Artistic Director of Ego Actus. She directed *I Know What Boys Want* at Theatre Row, *Six Characters in Search of an Author* in Oslo, Norway and *Kafka's Belinda* in Prague. She directed *Safe* and *what do you mean* at 59e59 in NYC and in the Edinburgh Festival Fringe. Joan has directed plays and readings for the Lark, Ensemble Studio Theatre, Theater for the New City, Urban Stages, and others. She won an Outstanding Direction Award and been nominated six times in MITF and Planet Connections. Joan was named to the **Indie Theatre Hall of Fame** by nytheatre.com. Joan has an MFA in Directing from The New School, an MS in Museum Education from Bank Street College.

Stacey Linnartz (director, **Section Two NEXT GENERATIONS**, and **CLOSING**; Artistic Coordinator) is Executive Producer of Third Wing Media, which produces film, online content and theatre in NYC, and is a Producer and Content Creator with Virtual Arts TV which streams live Off Broadway theatre. She is Artistic Director of Kids Creative Collective, a nonprofit arts organization which makes theatre in underserved NYC public schools. She is also an actor, select credits: *God of Vengeance* (The Barrow Group), *Moditti* (The Acorn/Theatre Row), *Amendment 13* (Clubbed Thumb), *Ghosting, Lost In Light* (The Public Theatre), *Heaven Can Wait* (Actors Studio). Regional: *Shipwrecked!* (Capital Rep), *Uncle Vanya* (New Harmony), *Eclectic Society* (Walnut Street), *As You Like It* (Smoky Mountain Shakespeare). London: *Old Times, Sirocco* (Royal Court). Film: *The Last 48, The Weekend, Shallow Point, The First Born, Godzilla.* Web: *First World problem, 12 Months of June.* MFA, NYU Graduate Acting Program.

Atonia Pettiford (director, **Section Four: BODY POL-ITICS**) directed *Girl Power, The Monologues of Teen Life* and *Voices of Africa* at Estrogenius Festivals of Manhattan Theatre Source. She develops after-school programs in theater for the Educational Alliance Boys and Girls Club, directing performance showcases. Atonia started her career as a model and actress, appearing in ads for Yoplait, NY Lottery, Johnson Hair Care, Glamour and more; serving as an on-air host for "E" Entertainment and others. Atonia is planning future theatrical productions with her sister, Tony-nominated actress Valarie Pettiford.

Melanie Sutherland (director, **Section Six: WHAT WE KNOW**): New York, regional, and university credits include new works to classics: *7 Sins in 60 Minutes (conceived/directed,* HERE/Philly Fringe*);A Pirate's Lullaby* (Jessica Litwak, Rattlestick); *Fargo* (David Morse, Circle Rep), *Easter in an Alley* (Michael Rispoli, Circle Rep); gender-bending *The Misanthrope* (AAI Prods); in development: *Vertical Village* (The Players); *Promised Land* (NJ Rep); *Marburg* (NYTW). John Golden Award; *Who's Who in the World, Who's Who in America, Who's Who of American Women, International Who's Who*. SDC.

Actors in the Reproductive Freedom Festival
Karmia Berry, Cameron Bossert, Anne Carney, Nikita Chaudhry, Kitty Chen, Francesca Choy-Kee, Gopal Divan, Amelia Fowler, Marisa Fratto, Amy Freinberg, Elise Gainer, Donnetta Lavinia Grays, Yvette Heyliger, Darlene Ivette, Jennifer J. Joseph, Carl H. Jaynes, Julia Kelly, Gina LeMoine, Stacey Linnartz, Jessica Litwak, Susan Maris, MacKenzie Meehan, Muriel Miguel, Mary Monahan, Lucio Nieto, Jeremy Rishe, Julissa Roman, Claudia Schneider, Hwalan Shub, Molly Stoller, Angelina Stokes, Lindsay Torrey, Kelly Vieau, and others.

Producing Team
The Reproductive Freedom Festival took place in New York City at TACT Studios in March 2016, and was live streamed by VirtualArts TV to all 50 state and 10 countries.

Production Manager, **Rachel Goddard;** Stage Manager, **Kelly Vieau**; Guests, Hosts: Adjoa Sankofia Tetteh, Malini Singh McDonald; Producing Assistance: Cameron Bossert, Susann Brinkley, Jenny Clarke, Zachary Rothman-Hicks, MacKenzie Meehan, Jeremy Rishe, Matthew Smith, International Women Artists Salon.

Graphics: **Jessica Noele DeWitt, Parid Cefa**

Project Support: The Puffin Foundation, Anne Hale and Arthur Johnson Fund, Abortion Conversations Project, and many individual donors.

SHORT PLAYS ON REPRODUCTIVE FREEDOM

CONTENTS:

SECTION ONE: HEROINES
Originally directed by Joan Kane

My Heroines by Marge Piercy
Lucky Old Lady by Marcy Arlin
Playground Placenta by Melissa Bell
Terrible Virtue by Jessica Litwak
Hardcore Latina Punk Birth Fragments by Grisel Acosta

MY HEROINES
by Marge Piercy

ABOUT THE PLAY: A poem

My Heroines

When I think of women heroes,
it's not Joan of Arc or Molly Pitcher
but mothers who quietly say
to their daughters, *you can.*
Who stand behind attempts
to open doors long bolted shut
to teams or clubs or professions.

I think of women who dress
'respectably' and march and march
and march again, for the ability
to choose, for peace, for rights
their own or others. Who form
phone banks, who stuff envelopes
who do the invisible political work.

They do not get their faces on
magazine covers. They don't get fan
mail or receive awards. But without
them, no woman or liberal man
would ever be elected, no law
would be passed or changed. We
would be stuck in sexist mud.

It's the receptionist in the clinic,
the escorts to frightened women,
the volunteers at no kill shelters,
women sorting bottles at the dump,
women holding signs in the rain,
women who take calls of the abused,
of rape victims, night after night.

It's the woman at her computer
or desk when the family's asleep
writing letters, organizing friends.
Big change turns on small pushes.
Heroes and heroines climb into
history books, but it's such women
who actually write our future.

The End

THE LUCKY OLD LADY
by Marcy Arlin

ABOUT THE PLAY

A monologue.

Setting: a warm, friendly room, anywhere. There is a large comfy chair center stage and a small table with a cup of coffee or tea or a brandy (depends on the actor) next to the chair. There should be some knickknacks, some hi-tech stuff. Imagine cushions, bowls of food for guests. Some cats or dogs wandering about.

Time: 100 years or so in the future.

The Lucky Old Lady

A very old lady sits in the comfortable chair, wearing a very futuristic shalwar jameez with a very old-fashioned afghan draped over the chair. She may wrap the afghan around her occasionally. She sips from her drink as warrants.

Welcome children. I am so happy to meet you all. My, there are a lot of you today. That is something special.

Yes, yes, I know you are not children. You are now newly and fully reproductive people. But, since I am 145 years old, you are children to me!

Before we start, I want to thank you for the gifts. But the truth is I really don't need any more figurines of extinct animals. Polar bears, otters, honey bees...it just makes me sad.

So congratulations! Now you may flirt and make love to your heart's content! But before you leave the crèche, you are required as you know, to hear this short talk by me, a certified historian of the early twenty-first century, specializing in women and reproduction. It is my job to tell you my story of the late Barbarian era so that you may see your lives in a true perspective.

It is my pleasure to let you know how very very lucky you all are.

When I was your age, back in the dark ages, some places on this watery planet of ours were good for women. Some were very very bad. Luckily I lived in a place that was good for some, with education, money, and living in a place that did not want to make life hard for women. Some places were just the opposite.

She takes a sip of liquid, sighs, looks away for a bit.

Today, so many years later, we have a very different society. For example, if you have a child, he or she will never starve or lack for an education or a chance to work at something wonderful. I know it's hard to believe that it was different.

To herself

Ah. The young...

But this is because of the tragedy of the Weather Wars. You learned about them from colleague, the ecology expert? Wonderful.

In those Wars, we lost so much. So many. So so many.

She pauses

But that is another story.

Before I start, I want to remind you that you are fortunate young people who can just program your implants to release fertile eggs or sperm. You can decide! No one can make you reproduce. Or not! If you want five children, or none, there is a place on earth.

But the past. Ah the past...

She stops. Pets a cat. Sips. Tries to remember.

Sorry, forgive an old woman. The memory refurbishing sometimes doesn't work as well as it should *(she laughs)*. So.

I was one of the last women for over forty years who had a choice about having a baby or not.

Do not gasp, my dears. Yes, about eighty years ago, the Family Together Laws were passed in what was then known as the United States. They said that women were not allowed to decide to have a child. Or not. Worse, Contraceptives were prohibited. If you had an abortion, you went to jail. Or worse.

But enough of that. You want to know my story! Before the Laws. Here it is.

I became pregnant by a man who beat me. I did not understand that I could leave him. Imagine!

I knew that if I had a child with him, he would never leave my life. I was afraid of him. He might steal and abuse a child. He was a poor sad person who had suffered terribly himself as a child. Once I pointed out that I hadn't tortured him. That earned me more punches and kicks.

Rightfully, now if someone beats you, their implants records it and they are put into a stasis. On the spot!!

So, I went to a doctor at a very good hospital. My baby, a fetus, was aborted at 8 weeks.

I will tell you the truth. I cried and cried for a long time. It was a horrible experience.

Then the man left me. Or I threw him out. I don't remember exactly what happened.

Years later, I married another man, a good man.

But in that ancient time, if you were over forty...Yes, 40!!!... as old as some of you children, fertility drained away and only if you had a lot of money and time could you get pregnant.

And then, under the Family Laws, because I had "given up" my first chance to have a child, I was forbidden to reproduce, even when the technology would let me.

Can you imagine?

(*She lets the 'children' talk among themselves for a bit.*)

We adopted a son and daughter. Who I love completely as only a good mother can.

But I will be honest with you. My children know this. Every so often I wonder what that baby would have been like. I feel sad and a little lonely.

(*She sits up straight and leans forward.*)

But make no mistake! I do not regret what I did, I did it to save my life and to save the child from a nightmare of an abusive father...

Many said to me: Women and men keep unwanted children, even with crazy spouses or poverty.

But at that time I had no family. No money. No job. If I was struggling with the child, and the child's father, I would not have become the teacher I became, teaching thousands of children to love and care and think.

Back then. I was fortunate. I had a choice.

The Laws. Such a sad time. Children pregnant after being raped by relatives or teachers. Women with five hungry children. One more meant no food or shelter for all of them. Women who were sick or emotionally unprepared. Women with bad spouses, male and female.

So many troubles. Wars, hunger, overpopulation. Violence, insanity. And then the Weather Wars. 4 billion people dead.

(*She pauses and covers herself with the afghan.*)

But as you have learned, the climate stabilized. We prospered again. Those who were left made good decisions.

The Family Laws disappeared.

And here you all are. Ready to leave the crèches and join all the men and women and creatures on this planet.

I give you all my love and good hopes.

(*The children leave.*)

Do not forget. Never forget.

The End

PLAYGROUND PLACENTA
by Melissa Bell

ABOUT THE PLAY

Character: Patti, a young mother into all things natural

Setting: Manhattan Plaza Playground, located between two tall buildings on W. 42nd St, between Ninth and Tenth Aves (in New York City)

Playground Placenta

PATTI

I would have so much more room in my freezer if it wasn't filled with placenta. No, not a natural hair conditioner. Real placenta. I had a home birth, and I kept Jake's placenta after he was born. The mid-wife got me into this idea of doing something with it. I want to bury it. Some cultures do that. It has something to do with nourishing the earth, giving life back into the ground.

You know that community garden on W.48th Street, the one between Ninth and Tenth? I wanted to bury it there, but I don't have a plot. So I asked this gay couple: "Can I bury my my son's placenta in your plot?" They just looked at me and said "No." Some cultures bury the boy's placenta under the threshold, and the girl's under the cornerstone ... or is it the girl's under the threshold? ... well ... I can't remember which goes where but you can't do that when you live in an apartment building. You're supposed to bury it in the place where they were born ... or where you want them to end up. You wouldn't want to get that wrong. Then I was thinking of putting it in the Hudson River ... you know, water, the giver of all life, but ..... naahh .... In some cultures they eat it, but my husband said no way. He wants me to throw it out, but I can't. I really want to do something with it. But it has been four years. Is there an expiration date?

The End

TERRIBLE VIRTURE
by Jessica Litwak

ABOUT THE PLAY

"It is only rebel woman, when she gets out of the habits imposed on her by bourgeois convention, who can do some deed of terrible virtue." – Margaret Sanger, **The Woman Rebel**

Terrible Virtue is a play about the history of reproductive rights in the U.S. and some of the ongoing and current cases of reproductive law.

The play is an ensemble for five women. Characters include Theresa (a fifteen-year-old pregnant girl in contemporary Kansas) her mother Bernadette, Norma McCovey, Emma Goldman, attorneys (from both sides), judges (Roe v. Wade and Margaret Sanger cases), Anthony Comstock, Geraldine (a female pastor in contemporary Kansas), Margaret Sanger, Sarah Weddington, teens, pharmacists, clinic staff, Horatio Storer, and others. The play goes back and forth between direct address, choral poetry and narrative scenes.

This excerpt is from the full-length play, and takes place in 1970 in a bar in Texas.
CHARACTERS
SARAH WEDDINGTON – A lawyer in Texas
ANDREA – A colleague of Sarah Weddington's
NORMA – 23 years old, living in Texas

Time and Place: 1970, A bar in Texas

Terrible Virtue

Lights shift, come up on a dimly lit rundown bar in the corner of town.

Andrea sits nervously tapping her fingers on a table in the corner of the room. The door opens and another woman in a suit appears, Weddington.

WEDDINGTON
Any word?

ANDREA
Not yet, but it's barely 8.

WEDDINGTON
How is she getting here?

ANDREA
She is borrowing her brother's truck.

WEDDINGTON
With or without his knowledge?

ANDREA
What are you so worried about?

WEDDINGTON
You told me she said he was a "punko," that he'd beat her up if he found out she was meeting us.

ANDREA
She'll be here.

34

WEDDINGTON
She seems stable to you?

ANDREA
She's a little high strung. But you wanted a white girl.

WEDDINGTON
This has to be about abortion and nothing more. We've only got one chance in Texas.

A young woman enters with disheveled clothes.

ANDREA
She's here. Relax. You'll frighten her off.

WEDDINGTON
(stands)
Hi Norma, I'm Sarah.

NORMA
Hey.

She sits. The other women sit.

WEDDINGTON
Would you like coffee or a coke?

NORMA
Can I have something to eat?

WEDDINGTON
Of course!

ANDREA
You know why we're here Norma?

NORMA
A slice of pizza or something.

ANDREA
Like I told you, we're looking for a woman to be a plaintiff in an abortion suit.

NORMA
What's a plaintiff?

WEDDINGTON
A plaintiff is the person bringing the case to trial- the one who is suing for something. In this case, you'd be suing for your right to get a legal abortion.

ANDREA
Tell her your story, Norma.

NORMA
You mean about joining the circus?

Weddington looks at Andrea. Norma laughs.

NORMA
Love the reaction that gets.

WEDDINGTON
I meant/ about-

NORMA
I'll get there. Anyway I got a job at a carnival. Selling tickets to the sideshow. I was into those freaky circus people. Tiny headed ape men, fat bearded women, kids with two faces. But I was mainly with the animals. Anyway.

We were doing our last night outside of a small town in Georgia, and a couple of roughnecks drinking too much caught up to us on our way back to the motel. My friends ran off but I wasn't so fast - the guys raped me, left me on the side of the road. When I woke up the carnival had left town and I didn't have a penny. I crawled back to Dallas, and pretty soon I started throwing up in the morning.

ANDREA
Did you go to a doctor?

NORMA
Yeah. First one said since I don't have maternal feelings, I must be sick in the head. Next one said all doubts will disappear when you see the baby. I told him I already got a kid lives with my mother, didn't want to see another baby. Third guy opened up the phonebook to the doctor page. Told me run my finger down the names. He goes "hot", "cold", "hot" like that, until I had my finger on a name. So I called him but he wanted two grand. One of my freako brother's friends set me up with a doctor in a motel, but the guy wanted to do the operation on the bathroom floor with a hanger. I wasn't letting that guy touch me.

ANDREA
Good.

NORMA
You had one?

ANDREA
What, an abortion? No?

NORMA
You?

WEDDINGTON
No.

NORMA
Then why you pushing so hard for this?

WEDDINGTON
I am a lawyer. I have tools not many women have access to.
I can do something for you and women like you.

NORMA
Women like me? Women who get themselves raped and the
circus leaves them behind?

ANDREA
Pregnant women who want to have the choice/ to

NORMA
I am not getting an abortion.

WEDDINGTON
You-?

NORMA
I mean I tried to. And I still might. But I just don't know if
it's the right thing or not. But tell you this. I sure do believe
I ought to have the right to have one. If I decided.

ANDREA
So you'll do it? You'll be our plaintiff?

NORMA
Well I don't know 'bout one thing. My family would sure
whop my butt if they found out I was going to court. I don't
know/if I can -

WEDDINGTON
You would be appearing in court under a different name.

NORMA
Oh. What name?

ANDREA
Jane.

WEDDINGTON
Jane Roe.

NORMA
Roe against who?

ANDREA
Mr. Henry Wade.

WEDDINGTON
He's the District Attorney of Dallas County. It would be us, be you, versus Wade.

NORMA
Roe versus Wade.

The lawyers nod. Norma smiles.

Blackout.

End of Excerpt

HARDCORE LATINA PUNK BIRTH FRAGMENTS
by Grisel Acosta

ABOUT THE PLAY

A Monologue

Setting: (if necessary) Urban bar.

Hardcore Latina Punk Birth Fragments

GRISEL

When someone says, "Latina," you get images of Salma Hayek, J-Lo, nowadays maybe even a graceful, ballet-trained Zoe Saldaña. You think of food and salsa dancing and accents, and no binge-watching time spent with April Ludgate on *Parks and Rec* can erase that insidiously indelible image. But we aren't all piñatas and mangos, for freak's sake. We are dark and precise like Borges' *Laberintos*, nerdy and cold like our Russian brethren who left us their names, bizarre and vicious like Al Jourgenson, el Cubano himself. My mother was dark, too, but she had no voice. Today, I am her voice. It goes beyond my tattoos and piercings. See, Mami had two boys; enough for her, she thought. No one bothered to tell my mother that she had to remove the IUD after a certain amount of time, so when several years had passed and she found herself pregnant with me, she was surprised. I grew in her belly despite the big murderous piece of plastic that was my roommate. My tiny limbs grew in a hostile environment in order to give my mother what she always wanted: a girl. She asked to not be sedated so that she could see my birth, but the doctors lied to her and conked her out anyway. Apparently, doctors at Mercy Hospital in Chicago don't give a shit about Cuban mothers, or their uteruses, or their daughters growing in their bellies, or their wishes, or simple pieces of infor-

40

mation that can make them happy, or saving their lives, or saving their daughter's lives. Mami accepted the disrespect silently. I was loud. And I fought. I fought to live in her womb, and then be born, and only a few months later, during the Christmas and New Year holiday, I fought to live despite becoming sick with pneumonia. My father sat in the hospital with me as I cried and cried in pain from within a crib encased in plastic. He could only insert his hand through a rubber glove to touch me and I grabbed his thumb and, according to the story he always tells, I did not want to let go. The hospital did not allow him or my mother to stay with me overnight. They hated to leave me, but I survived. By the time I was four months old, I had kicked death's ass twice. I was *born* a punk. One year, when I'm not 10 years old yet, I dress up as a punk for Halloween. I wear a trash bag as a dress and belt it with my mom's wide purple fabric belt with a rhinestone buckle. I get the idea from European music videos on the MV3 channel, videos about chauffeurs and cannibals. My afro is sprayed with orange and pink hair color, my lipstick is black and my eyes are outlined in silver. The picture Tía takes of me, in the room we share, is full-length; I stand with my hand on my hip, head cocked to one side and the attitude on my face is deadly...and pretty funny silly *(laughs)*. The next year, I am the ghost of a motorcycle biker who had a terrible accident. I wear denim jeans and a jacket, a raggedy white T-shirt, a pull-on mask that is gruesome, a denim hat and knee-high boots. Papi keeps asking what I am because he doesn't understand my costume and it makes me furious that I have to keep telling him. Deep down, I am furious because he would have understood a Miss Universe costume better. But that's okay. I know. Even Miss Universe herself -- who's *always* Latina *(sighs)* — knows that under the sequins and paint, we are hardcore chicas, always taking advantage of your underestimation, always fighting for ownership of our bodies, ownership of our lives. And winning.

Blackout

End of Play

SECTION TWO: NEXT GENERATIONS
Originally directed by Stacey Linnartz

The Pill by Laura Zlatos
Two Girls by Allie Costa
Women and ...? by Angela Bonavoglia
In the Service we said and **Women's Liberation** by Judith Arcana

---

THE PILL
by Laura Zlatos

ABOUT THE PLAY
Character Name - Gender

Erin – F
Pharmacist – M
Man – M
Man 2 –M
Man 3 – M
Man 4 – M
Teenager – M
Cop – M

The play was performed in the Reproductive Freedom Festival by four actors, two male (one as the pharmacist, one other men), two female (one as Erin, one as other men)

The Pill

A pharmacy. There are a line of people waiting to pick up prescriptions. Erin stands at the front.

PHARMACIST
Next!
Erin walks up to the pharmacist.
Name.

ERIN
Erin Moffat. M-O-F-F-A-T.
The pharmacist looks through the prescriptions under M and finds Erin's.

PHARMACIST
Next!

ERIN
It's still my turn.

PHARMACIST
We don't sell that here.

ERIN
Birth control?

PHARMACIST
Next!

A man steps up.

MAN
I have a prescription for cocaine.

PHARMACIST
One minute.

ERIN
I'm sorry, what?

43

PHARMACIST
You're holding up the line.

The pharmacist gives the man cocaine. Man 2 steps up.

ERIN
I'm not leaving until you give me my prescription.

MAN 2
Do you carry anthrax?

PHARMACIST
Of course.

The pharmacist gives man 2 anthrax. Man 3 steps up.

ERIN
You sell anthrax, but you won't sell birth control?

PHARMACIST
Birth control kills.

MAN 3
I called in about an AK-47.

PHARMACIST
Are you sure you don't want the F2000 assault rifle? More rounds per minute and it comes with a grenade launcher.

MAN 3
Why not?

The pharmacist gives man 3 an assault rifle.

ERIN
You literally just handed him a loaded gun.

PHARMACIST
How could I be so stupid? Sir, I forgot to give you the bullets.

MAN 3
That was close.

PHARMACIST
It won't happen again.

Man 3 leaves.

ERIN
That's definitely illegal.

PHARMACIST
Get out of my line!

ERIN
Look, I saw my gynecologist, she wrote me a prescription, and I called it in. Why won't you just hand it over and I'll be on my way?

PHARMACIST
Next!

Man 4 steps up.

MAN 4
I'm picking up a black rhino.

ERIN
You don't mean a real black rhino, do you?

MAN 4
Yes, I do.

ERIN
But don't they live in Africa? And aren't they endangered?

The pharmacist gives man 4 a black rhino.

PHARMACIST
Last one.

Man 4 leaves.

ERIN
You're giving that man the last black rhino on earth? You're wiping out an entire species, but you won't give me birth control?

PHARMACIST
Next!

A teenage boy steps up in a tuxedo.

TEENAGER
I'm here to pick up my date to the prom.

ERIN
You realize this is a pharmacy, don't you? And he won't even give me birth control so I seriously doubt he'll give you-

PHARMACIST
Here she is.

The pharmacist gives the teenager a very unhappy teenage girl in a prom dress. The boy ushers her away.

ERIN
You can't do that! I'm gonna call the cops.

A cop steps up.

COP
I'd like the Millennium Falcon.

ERIN
Can you please help me? I'm trying to pick up my birth control and this man won't let me take it.

COP
Why would you wanna take birth control?

ERIN
To be a responsible woman who has some agency over the way I live my life.

COP
That's ridiculous.

PHARMACIST
Here you go.

She's right outside.
The cop leaves.

ERIN
That's not even real!

Beat.

Look, I don't tell you how to live your life so why don't you stop telling me how to live mine?

PHARMACIST
Next!

Man 5 steps up.

MAN 5
I need something for my penis. So that I can have a lot of sex with a lot of different women. At the same time and separately.

PHARMACIST
Viagra?

MAN 5
Don't need it.

PHARMACIST
Condoms?

MAN 5
Don't want it.

PHARMACIST
I know just the thing.

The pharmacist gives him a rectangular box.

It's a second penis. It's guaranteed to double the amount of women you inseminate.

MAN 5
I can't believe I've been living all my life with just one.

He leaves.

ERIN
You've got to be kidding me.

PHARMACIST
Next!

ERIN
There's no one left in line.

Beat.
I'm not asking for a lot. I'm not asking for an assault weapon or an illicit drug or a penis-- in fact, I think we have enough of those in the world, but that's besides the point. I'm asking you to put yourself in my shoes. To think about what it would be like to sacrifice your body and alter the course of your life for something you're not ready for or something you may never want. I'm asking you to look at me as a person. Just like you.

PHARMACIST
Next!

End of Play

TWO GIRLS
by Allie Costa

ABOUT THE PLAY

Dramatis Personae

Girl One: Late teens to 30s. Seemingly put-together. Any ethnicity.

Girl Two: Same age as Girl One. Slightly bolder. Any ethnicity.

NOTE: The actresses address the audience rather than each other, and their voices are distinctly different, but there is a synchronicity, a rhythm in the words and intention that keeps the piece flowing seamlessly from start to finish.

Two Girls

At Rise:
The stage is dark. We hear the sounds of the highway at a distance, mixed with nature: a passing car, a dove, a slight breeze whistling through the trees.

Lights slowly rise, flickering. Two women stand single-file center stage, with GIRL ONE directly in front of GIRL TWO. Their outfits may be similar, even identical, or very different. GIRL ONE has carefully applied makeup, a nice hairstyle, cute shoes. GIRL TWO is barefoot, disheveled. Both of their heads are bowed. The stage is bare.

As the lights come up – not quite full, still somewhat brown – and the sounds dim, GIRL ONE lifts her head and addresses the audience:

GIRL ONE
One girl entered the forest.

The girls split apart and stand shoulder to shoulder as GIRL TWO tells us:

GIRL TWO
Another girl left it.

GIRL ONE
She wasn't reckless.

GIRL TWO
She wasn't careless.

50

GIRL ONE
She just wanted to get home.

GIRL TWO
She just wanted to get some sleep.

GIRL ONE
She'd walked that path a hundred times before.

GIRL TWO
A thousand times.

GIRL ONE
But they weren't there before.

GIRL TWO
This time, they were.

GIRL ONE
They called out to her.

GIRL TWO
They whistled.

GIRL ONE
She ignored them.

GIRL TWO
Ignore them and they'll go away.

GIRL ONE
Keep walking.

GIRL TWO
Don't stop.

The girls take a few steps apart. Throughout the piece, the girls take a few steps apart every so often, the shuddering light lengthening to match the width of their movement.

GIRL ONE
She heard footsteps behind her.

GIRL TWO
She walked faster.

GIRL ONE
She wasn't fast enough.

GIRL TWO
They stopped her.

GIRL ONE
He was in front of her.

GIRL TWO
Behind her.

GIRL ONE
Surrounding her.

GIRL TWO
There were two of them.

GIRL ONE
Or three.

GIRL TWO
Or four.

GIRL ONE
Or just one. It doesn't matter.

GIRL TWO
It doesn't matter how many.

GIRL ONE
He was bigger.

GIRL TWO
He was stronger.

GIRL ONE
She had her keys threaded through her fingers.

GIRL TWO
That didn't help.

GIRL ONE
The keys didn't protect her.

GIRL TWO
They got lost in the struggle.

GIRL ONE
She took a self-defense class one time.

GIRL TWO
She had taken self-defense classes for three years.

GIRL ONE
She never thought this would happen to her.

GIRL TWO
She never thought this could happen to her.

GIRL ONE begins to pull at her clothes nervously.
GIRL TWO tries to straighten hers.

GIRL ONE
She wasn't prepared.

GIRL TWO
She thought she was prepared.

GIRL ONE
She was having a good day.

GIRL TWO
It had been a long day.

GIRL ONE
It was daytime.

GIRL TWO
It was nighttime.

GIRL ONE
She was wearing a brand-new dress.

GIRL TWO
She was wearing jeans.

GIRL ONE
She was wearing high heels.

GIRL TWO
She was wearing running shoes.

GIRL ONE
It doesn't matter what she was wearing.

GIRL TWO
It doesn't matter what time of day it was.

GIRL ONE
All that matters is that it happened.

GIRL TWO
It happens every day.

GIRL ONE
Every two minutes.

GIRL TWO
It feels like it lasts forever.

GIRL ONE
She was in the suburbs.

GIRL TWO
She was downtown.

GIRL ONE
She was two blocks from home.

GIRL TWO
She was on her way to work.

GIRL ONE
It doesn't matter where she was.

GIRL TWO
It doesn't matter where she had been.

GIRL ONE
It doesn't matter where she was going.

GIRL TWO
She didn't get there in time.

GIRL ONE
He didn't carry a weapon.

GIRL TWO
He *was* a weapon.

GIRL ONE
She couldn't speak.

GIRL TWO
She screamed at the top of her lungs.

GIRL ONE
Her heart was in her throat.

GIRL TWO
He laughed at her.

GIRL ONE
He said nothing.

GIRL TWO
The things they said...

GIRL ONE
She couldn't hear.

GIRL TWO
He looked like her uncle.

GIRL ONE
Her co-worker.

GIRL TWO
Someone you'd see at the grocery store.

GIRL ONE
On the subway.

GIRL TWO
At the PTA.

GIRL ONE
A friend.

GIRL TWO
A stranger.

GIRL ONE
She couldn't see.

GIRL TWO
It was too dark.

GIRL ONE
She closed her eyes and waited for it to be over.

GIRL TWO
She fought back. She drew blood.

GIRL ONE
She wanted it to be over.

GIRL TWO
She wanted it to be over.

GIRL ONE
...And then it was.

GIRL TWO
And then she was alone.

GIRL ONE
Except she wasn't.

GIRL TWO
She'll never be alone again.

GIRL ONE
They are in her head, all the time.

GIRL TWO
He's always in the back of her mind.

GIRL ONE
When she's on a date with someone new.

GIRL TWO
When she's in a dark parking lot.

GIRL ONE
When she closes her eyes at night.

GIRL TWO
She remembers.

GIRL ONE
She can't forget.

GIRL TWO
She'll never forget.

GIRL ONE
One girl entered the forest.

GIRL TWO
Another girl left it.

GIRL ONE
She searches every day.

GIRL TWO
She looks for the girl she used to be.

GIRL ONE
She catches glimpses of her sometimes.

GIRL TWO
In the mirror.

GIRL ONE
When she's not looking.

GIRL TWO
When she's not trying.

GIRL ONE
In the morning.

The light warms up, just a touch. The two girls take steps towards each other, slowly. They may still be addressing the audience; they might finally be addressing each other. Either way, they are talking to themselves now.

GIRL TWO
When she's singing.

GIRL ONE
When she's laughing.

GIRL TWO
When she's living.

GIRL ONE
There she is.

GIRL TWO
She's still there.

GIRL ONE
She's still here.

GIRL TWO
She's not ashamed.

GIRL ONE
Stand tall.

GIRL TWO
Keep walking.

GIRL ONE
Don't stop.

GIRL TWO
Don't stop.

The girls look forward, GIRL ONE hopeful, GIRL TWO determined, and take a collective breath –

Blackout

End of Play

WOMEN AND...?
by Angela Bonavoglia

ABOUT THE PLAY

A monologue.

Adapted from an essay by the writer, originally published in the magazine *Conscience* from Catholics for Choice.

Women and ...?

It's hard to say this out loud, because I don't know how it will be taken, but I have never wanted to have children.
I grew up in an Italian, Catholic, working-class town teeming with kids. But I recall no fantasies of motherhood. The weariness of my maternal grandma's body, bloated from the burden of eleven births, was palpable. Childbirth killed my paternal grandmother, and I'm one of her namesakes. My mother had just two children. Born into a large, poor family, she knew what it felt like to be accidental, one among too many. She thought children should be no accident, that they should be invited, wanted, absolutely longed for. For me, that longing never came, but she didn't measure my worth by that.

I used to think that because I didn't want to have kids, I had to show all the other ways I'd mothered that had nothing to do with biology. I'd say that I did my mothering growing up, when my mother, brother and I took care of each other after my father died. I'd say that I'd done my mothering as a therapist; as the "othermother" to a wonderful girl who is now herself a mother; and as a writer, by bringing women's voices out into the world.

All that is true. But I don't feel that I need to defend myself with that litany anymore.

You see, being "childless" can inspire a whole range of negative reactions in people, from befuddlement to pity to resentment. The language doesn't help. I've always hated the term "child-less," implying, as it does, some devastating deficit, like being heartless. I much prefer "child-free," which I've seen bandied about but dare not use, implying as *it* does some pride in my uncommon state.

Which makes me wonder: Why is it so hard to have women among us who don't want to be mothers?

I think it's because motherhood is seen as a woman's major rite of passage. Having babies earns us trust. It takes the edge off our suspect sexuality. But what is the culture to make of a woman who rejects that rite of passage? Who does not want to have a child? If women are capable of rejecting that role, of not loving in that way, then we might be capable of *anything*.

And that's scary.

A woman, childless by choice, standing alone, remains strange and unfamiliar. Who is she? What does she want? Is she safe? Is she good?

Rather than find out the answers to those questions, desperate men the world over do everything in their power to make the decision to reject motherhood as difficult as possible, thereby keeping the two safely cemented, as almost one word: **womenandchildren.**

The End

IN THE SERVICE WE SAID
and
WOMEN'S LIBERATION
by Judith Arcana

ABOUT THE PLAY: The selections are two poems. In the Reproductive Freedom Festival, it was performed by three actors.

In the Service we said

In the Service we spoke clearly and distinctly:
We said, This is Jane from Women's Liberation;
please leave your name, your number and a message.
We'll call you back. When she did, we did; then
we said, What was the date of your last period?

When we met to talk, we said, Are you sure
you want to do this? When she said Yes,
we said syringe, speculum, dilator, curette;
we said vagina, we said cervix, we said uterus,
telling how to open it from the outside;
sometimes we had to say forceps, placenta, labor,
trimester, hours, contractions, fetus.

(To each other, learning, we said it feels like
the roof of your mouth, those ridges up in there;
the curette scrapes along those ridges, spoonlike.
We said you can feel the shape, like a textbook
illustration; it feels just like the picture looks,
it feels just like you think it will; that helps. Later,
sometimes we said, She was more afraid of the shot
than anything else. Or we said, Her cervix was so tight,
I thought I'd be there for an hour, my arm frozen,
my shoulder numb, holding that dilator still.)

Lying there, some would ask, so we said No,
we're not doctors; we're women just like you.

We needed to know how, so we learned it –
you know, just like you learn anything.

Women's Liberation
(*... for Esther*)

Every week we went to a meeting,
but not like now. No one stood up
and said, My name is Jane and I'm
an abortionist. No. Because we didn't
want to stop, we weren't trying not to do it.
We sat in apartments, passing the cards.

One card is Sandy from West Lafayette,
eighteen years old, coming in on the bus.
She's got about sixty-three dollars, she thinks
she's nine weeks pregnant. The next card is
Terrelle, who's thirty-two and angry. Her
doctor gave her an IUD that didn't work;
he says there's nothing he can do.
Here's Mona, fifty-four years old, has one
hundred dollars, wants to keep this secret
from her family. And Carlie, a long term –
twenty weeks pregnant, may have ten dollars,
twelve years old like Mona's youngest – she
got herpes from her brother when he did it.

Every week some of the cards were passed
around for hours; none of us wanted
to counsel those women, take one
into her life. The longest of long terms,
they lived far away, had no one but us,
no one to tell, no one to help, no money.
They needed everything. Cards went around
the room while we talked: dilation, syringes,
xylocaine, the Saturday list. At the end
of the meeting, all the cards were taken.

The End

SECTION THREE: CONFLICTS
Originally directed by Francesca Mantani Arkus

Certain Doom by Stephen Cedars
Cobra This! by Jeremy Rishe
American Girl/Igbo World by Junita Middleton
Rhymes with Ryan (On the Hill 2016) by Cindy Cooper

CERTAIN DOOM
by Stephen Cedars

ABOUT THE PLAY

Characters
Wife, F, 30's-40's, a strong-willed peasant women unaware of her own strength
Husband, M, 30's a well-meaning but ineffectual peasant
Daughter, F, 16-20, a free-spirited peasant
Bishop, M, 30's-40's, an arrogant authority dressed in full garb, maybe even with a silly hat

Place
A peasant's hovel.

Time
Not so long ago as we'd like to believe...

Certain Doom

HUSBAND paces wildly, as WIFE watches with concern.

HUSBAND
Oh heavens oh heavens I tell you wife, we are indeed in a pickle, spelling no doubt certain doom unless...oh we are doomed!

WIFE
Do shut yer hole husband and spell out for me the calamity.

HUSBAND
OK, ok, very well. I, um - oh dear -

WIFE
DO BUSTLE YER BALLS TOGETHER AND TELL ME.

HUSBAND
Our daughter is with child!

He CRIES out, into his hands. She takes it in.

WIFE
Our daughter is unmarried.

HUSBAND
I do know it!

WIFE
I knew she fancied the smith's son but...

HUSBAND
She does love him, deeming that ample, ah, she's always been of too free a spirit, oh my!

WIFE
Well shit. It's a pickle indeed. May be some might one call backwards this world of ours so entrenched as it is in stifling Christian penance and shame. But for today, tis what

tis, and what tis has little compassion for such so-deemed sinfulness.

HUSBAND
And us being poor, we've no options for clever restitutions or speargun weddings like the barons might have. And of course...that is, even should she want to end the condition...

WIFE
Don't even mention it! That indeed would mean we're toast no kidding.

DAUGHTER
Atop of which I got me no hankering for such violence.

The daughter bounds on. Mom pulls her hair.

WIFE
You fool, do you know we are doomed?!

DAUGHTER
Mama, please!

HUSBAND
Show mercy, dear woman!

WIFE
Mercy? Yer the man of the family. Was you was meant to scare the girl to straightness, was you too wormy to do it, now's it me crossed a line?

HUSBAND
Ay, perhaps my too liberal thought is to blame. I thought it only fair each person ought be allowed her own way of living and thinking, that she should pursue happiness, but now - !

DAUGHTER
Don't apologize for that! Tis Papa's way of thinking has made me happy, be sure!

Mom stops, looks between them.

WIFE
Yah well tis Papa's way done damned us all then. Ya know it I've always admired yer sprit too, darling, it's the like of which I never coulda claimed for myself, but hogshead, we are plum screwed now.

DAUGHTER
Perhaps it is we all stand together, and tell the church to scram.

HUSBAND
No no, no need for such aggression, we ought push more gradual, talk plain our case and -

DAUGHTER
Do man up, papa.

WIFE
We all are who we are, girl. And we as ladies ain't got no leg from which to fight.

She takes a cross, HITS a bell with it. It RINGS.

DAUGHTER
No, please - !

HUSBAND
Hold, let's us talk it through first –!

WIFE
Best we all admit what's in charge and cross our fingers for mercy -

A fully-garbed BISHOP enters.

BISHOP
You rang?

WIFE
(after a moment, in a whisper)
...Husband, step forward!

BISHOP
You rang?!

WIFE
Get yer ass forward and advocate, damnit!

She pushes him forward.

HUSBAND
Uh sure, yer holiness, we was just, we wanted to, thinking most of personal freedoms and, uh, dignity owed -

The bishop begins smelling the air like a bloodhound.

BISHOP
I sense a certain stench of...Yes there is something afoot.... something...

He smells the girl's belly, and pervily feels around it.

BISHOP
Aha! Oh, this is unfortunate. A girth two kopits disproportionate but lacking a ring...

WIFE
Perhaps yer holiness, we can simply tell ya the news, ya
need not, um, use your hands so -

BISHOP
You accuse me of disrespect?! Tis you who have disre-
spected your daughter's body, wench! I in my capacity am
concerned only with its godly nature.

*He feels her all over again, then turns to husband as the
women whisper to each other.*

DAUGHTER
Mama, I feel unclean...

WIFE
I know it, dear, but be strong...

DAUGHTER
Why do you not confront him? You know Papa is unable
despite his noble intentions -

WIFE
Ours is a patriarchy, dear, so it must fall to yer papa to
stand up, ineffectual as he might be.

BISHOP
Very well. She is to be publicly shamed, the child's to be
born and she to be married, and you taxed heavily for the
sanctity such will endow on the ceremony.

HUSBAND
I respectfully, isn't that all a bit, I dunno, harsh, yer holiness -

WIFE
Stand up for her, man!

HUSBAND
Um, I wonder if mayhaps my daughter might be best served controlling her own situation?

BISHOP
Poppycock! The sinful wench is to deliver the child under the watchful eye of yours truly!

WIFE
Shit no!

BISHOP
Excuse me?!

WIFE
...nothing. Was not my place to speak.

BISHOP
So it is settled.

DAUGHTER
Mama! Papa's no idea how terrible this truly is - you must fight!

WIFE
Alas dear, we are reliant on others to fight our fight...

BISHOP
(pulling on a glove)
Now - I will conduct the first sanctified study of the girl's body. Come along.

He starts to pull her out of the room.

DAUGHTER
Please, mama, please - !

WIFE
Husband, you must do something!

HUSBAND
Mine ideas don't sanction rebellion, sadly, and -

DAUGHTER
Mama, it's to you! It's to you! Find the balls that papa lacks!

HUSBAND
A fair insult, sadly.

WIFE
I ... darling, I can't ... I don't ...

BISHOP
Do shut it, slut, and accept that your body belongs to us!

WIFE
(suddenly enlivened)
Don't you call my daughter a slut!

She grabs the priest by his cloak, yanks him back.

BISHOP
Wha - ?

WIFE
Listen here, you sanctimonious shit, yer time's coming to its end. Me girl will have her baby if and as she pleases, she'll marry if and when it strikes, and if ya cares not for it, you can kiss my ass!

She throws him out of the room. A moment, then:

DAUGHTER
Mama! What nerve, what fire!

HUSBAND
My, that was something –

WIFE
What inspired foolishness, I think ya means. Come family, let's us hold each other tight. Such bravery will cost us dear...

They gather around her, and she holds them close.

DAUGHTER
And yet others will see and follow and triumph!

WIFE
Indeed we hope. We'll suffer now for the truth and hope, hope that what's clear as day might soon be seen as such, that folks might keep their grubbies off of where it don't belong, that this all too rigid world of hypocritical bullshit soon might pass....

DAUGHTER
Sure enough it will. For now, let's all simply love one another.

HUSBAND
Sounds good.

End of Play.

COBRA THIS!
by Jeremy Rishe

ABOUT THE PLAY

CHARACTERS
Casey On The Phone – a health insurance consultant who answers questions by phone
Raymore – a health consumer
Phone operator – A person fielding general phone calls

At Rise:
A Living Room

RAYMONE kneels with his iPad. He dials a number on his cellphone. RING... RING... RI-

PHONE OPERATOR
Local Eleven Seventeen Pension and Health, what is your Union ID Number?

RAYMONE
Hi. How are you?

PHONE OPERATOR
Fine, what is your Union ID Number?

RAYMONE
473446.

Silence. Silence. Silence.

PHONE OPERATOR
Hello *Raymon.*

RAYMONE
Ray*mone.*

PHONE OPERATOR
I'm sorry. Raymone, how can I help you?

RAYMONE
Yes, my wife is pregnant. And I'm concerned we might loose our Health Insurance. It seems the number of days I worked was miscounted. It -

PHONE OPERATOR
You're calling about an error on your earnings record?

RAYMONE
Um...yes-

PHONE OPERATOR
Please hold.

The song Spiral Dance, by Keith Jarrett, plays from the phone. Raymone grooves with the music. Until...

PHONE OPERATOR
Raymone? I have Casey from Adjustments on the line. Casey, Ray mone had a concern with the number of days he worked. If you don't need anything else I'm going to hang up... Ok? Thank you, Ray mone! - (click)

CASEY ON THE PHONE
Hello Raymone, what seems to be your problem?

RAYMONE
Yes- It shows online that I only worked 7.3 days in the last 8 months -

CASEY ON THE PHONE
Ok...?

RAYMONE
I worked more than that...I think what happened is the days the earnings were *reported* were counted; rather than the *actual days worked*.

CASEY ON THE PHONE
I see. Do you have a copy of the contract?

RAYMONE
(trying to remember)
... I... might.

CASEY ON THE PHONE
If you can e-mail a copy of your contract to R-A-C-H-E-L@E-L-E-V-E-N-S-E-V-E-N-T- E-E-N.COM that's CASEY@ELEVENSEVENTEEN.COM

RAYMONE
R-A-G-?

CASEY ON THE PHONE
R-A-C-H-E-L@ELEVENSEVENTEEN.COM

RAYMONE
R-A-C-H-E-L...?

CASEY ON THE PHONE
@ELEVENSEVENTEEN.COM

RAYMONE
RACHEL@ELEVENSEVENTEEN.COM .

CASEY ON THE PHONE
Yes.

RAYMONE
Not CASEY...

CASEY ON THE PHONE
No. Is that all I can help you with?

RAYMONE
I'm just curious, why my union doesn't have a copy of the contract?

CASEY ON THE PHONE
We are not your Union.

RAYMONE
... Who am I talking to?

CASEY ON THE PHONE
Local Eleven Seventeen Pension and Health.

RAYMONE
Right...

CASEY ON THE PHONE
You're Union is Local 11/17. We are Local Eleven Seventeen Pension and Health.
We are separate; we do not share information, for legal reasons. That's why you need to email a copy of the contract in question, if you have one, to casey@eleven-

RAYMONE
Casey???@elevenseventeen-?

CASEY ON THE PHONE
No!!! Rachel!!! - I'm sorry - Rachel@elevenseventeen.com. Like I spelled it out for you.

RAYMONE
Rachel...

CASEY ON THE PHONE
Yes. That is correct. Is there anything else I can help y ou with?

RAYMONE
What if I don't have a copy of the contract?

CASEY ON THE PHONE
The union should be able to provide you with one.

RAYMONE
Then can't they provide you with one?

CASEY ON THE PHONE
I'm sorry, they cannot.

RAYMONE
Oh... I see.

CASEY ON THE PHONE
Only Union members can request their own personal information.

RAYMONE
What was that?

CASEY ON THE PHONE
Only union members can request their own information.

RAYMONE
Just not from you?

CASEY ON THE PHONE
We are contracted out by the Union. We do share a similar name, but that is for the sake of ease in administering between the Union, its members, and the health insurance –

RAYMONE
Not very well.

CASEY ON THE PHONE
... Is there anything else I can help you with today?

RAYMONE
Yeah, get a copy of my contract from the Union whose name you share- I send you money every quarter-

CASEY ON THE PHONE
We do not disseminate health insurance. We administrate-

RAYMONE
I know this!!!

CASEY ON THE PHONE
What else can I help you with today, Raymone?

RAYMONE
Don't call me by my first name! Call me by my sur name?

Casey laughs. Raymone waits.

CASEY ON THE PHONE
What is your last name?

RAYMONE
You don't have it there-?

CASEY ON THE PHONE
No sir, your last name is kept blank to us, for your privacy.

RAYMONE
You know, my wife is pregnant. If we lose our health in-surance, because of a stupid clerical error, that's it. We're done! Financially!!

CASEY ON THE PHONE
We do have a Cobra option. -

RAYMONE
Do you know how expensive Cobra is??

CASEY ON THE PHONE
I don't set the premiums, but I can access your record to take a look-

RAYMONE
So you do have my record on file? ... ... How many days does it show I worked?

CASEY ON THE PHONE
Can you give me your union ID number?

RAYMONE
Again??

CASEY ON THE PHONE
You never gave to me, and I'm going to need it in order to access that part of your-

RAYMONE
4 7 3 4 4 6!

CASEY ON THE PHONE
Ok. So you want to know how many days you worked?

RAYMONE
I worked 63 days since April, but my earnings record shows 7.3.

CASEY ON THE PHONE
That is correct, 7.3 days.

RAYMONE
Right, and that is wrong.

CASEY ON THE PHONE
I should inform you, as well, that none of the things we are talking about now can be looked into until your eligibility period ends.

RAYMONE
Wait-What?? After my eligibility period ends? It will be too late. I'm trying-... that's two months from now, two and half months. I'm trying to avoid a stressful situation for me and my pregnant wife - so she can stick with the same OBGYN doctor -

CASEY ON THE PHONE
We are not your health insurance provider, we administer eligibility and payments.

RAYMONE
Look, this is your problem-

CASEY ON THE PHONE
This sounds like you and your pregnant wife's problem.

RAYMONE
(silence, silence, silence)

(silence)

What did you say to me?

CASEY ON THE PHONE
I'm sorry , you broke up there...

RAYMONE
You said this is my pregnant wife's problem.

CASEY ON THE PHONE
We only respond to the information we are given.

RAYMONE
What??? I'm telling you, you were given the right information and did the wrong thing with it.

CASEY ON THE PHONE
Are you referring to your earnings record or the comment I made about your wife?

RAYMONE
You know what? I don't trust this union has my best interest -

CASEY ON THE PHONE
We are not your Un-

RAYMONE
I don't think this health insurance company wants to pay for the service -

CASEY ON THE PHONE
We are not your hea-

RAYMONE
I don't even think I need health insurance!

CASEY ON THE PHONE
Well, you don't have a choice any more.

RAYMONE
What if I choose to take my money and pay the doctor directly?

CASEY ON THE PHONE
Well, that's certainly a radical idea.

RAYMONE
It's rational. My idea is rational, it's reasonable. It's the way it always was, for nearly ALL of humanity, until recently!!

CASEY ON THE PHONE
Is there anything else I can help you with today?

RAYMONE
Go fuck yourself!

CASEY ON THE PHONE
Thank you so much for calling Local Eleven Seventeen Pension and Health, can you please hang up the phone now?

RAYMONE
You're a completely useless piece of shit! *You* hang up the phone!

CASEY ON THE PHONE
FCC regulations do not allow me to disconnect the call. You must disconnect the call.

RAYMONE
Oh really? Well, that's not my problem!

Raymone drops his phone and leaves the room.

CASEY ON THE PHONE
Raymone? Are you still there?
(As the lights fade, the phone on the floor.)
Raymone? .... Can you please disconnect the call.... Raymone...? Raymone...? Raymone...

Fade to black.

The End

AMERICAN GIRL, IGBO WORLD
by Junita Middleton

ABOUT THE PLAY

A Monologue

American Girl, Igbo World

Igbolachi! My name is Nkiruka Chikwem and I am a Nigerian-American. In the Igbo culture, our names hold very valuable meaning. My name means, "The best is yet to come." I would like to believe this is true, however, my life may not be defined by my name after all. I am four weeks pregnant by the man of my dreams, Jamal Dixon. We are madly in love and he has asked me to marry him multiple times. As much as I want to say yes and would have the first time he proposed, I can not. I am marrying another man a few months after my college graduation.

Even though I live in America and follow many American traditions, my family is originally from Nigeria. Both my parents come from Badia East, a slum built on a marshy landfill in Lagos. They have never had much, but always managed to get by. Even in America, we are still getting by. My father doesn't want me or any of my siblings to live just getting by. He has decided to take it upon himself to set up an arranged marriage. Because I am an American, studying medicine in college, and considered to be the most beautiful of my sisters, plenty of men have asked to marry me. My father has turned down many, but he has found an older Nigerian man who comes from one of the wealthier towns called Harcourt. This area is surrounded by oil money so this man is rich.

Maybe another woman would be ecstatic about leaving the world of struggle to marry a rich man and would never have to worry again, but not me. I am already rich with love, good health, and happiness with Jamal. If only I could tell my father that. In most Nigerian homes, the father is the head of the household and whatever he says goes. Jamal has asked me to run away with him and start our own life knowing the fear that I have for my father, but I could never do that. No one knows about Jamal besides my closest sister. If my father was to find out I secretly had a boyfriend I know he would not be happy. If he were to find out I was having intercourse there would be an issue. If he were to find out I was pregnant, there would be an even bigger issue. But if he were to find out I was getting an abortion, that would be an issue that I could not never return from. Religion plays a central role in a Nigerians' daily life. Abortion is considered a huge sin and with my family's strong Christian faith, I would be cursed and told I am going straight to hell along with being disowned. I could not live with that guilt. On the other hand, being that I am pregnant out of wedlock with a Black- American, my arranged marriage would have to be stopped. It would seem as if I refused to marry and I would still be disowned. I would miss my mother and my siblings way too much. With me just finding out about the pregnancy and only being 4 weeks, I do not have a connection with my baby like I do with them.

Once I graduate and get accepted into a Medical university in Lagos, my entire family and I will be flying out to Nigeria. I have a huge decision to make before then. If I were still living in Nigerian and I were in the same situation, I wouldn't have a choice at all. Nigeria is the second most religious country in the world. There is a deep stigma around abortion. Abortion is legally restricted unless it is to save the woman's life. Many women, especially women who live in the villages like mine can not afford a child, so they find clinics that perform abortions under the table. This takes a great risk because most of these providers who perform such procedures do not have proper training nor do they work in a setting that meets medical standards. With that being said, women end up in conditions that lead to hemorrhaging, fever, sepsis, infection of the bowels or uterus, and/or even death. Here in the United States, abortions are legal and the mortality is close to none. The professionals are licensed and trained correctly. They also have the proper equipment. According to reports by the Guttmacher Institute and the government of Nigeria, even though abortions are illegal, at least 760,000 abortions happen every year, and from 3,000 to 34,000 women die annually from unsafe procedures. With my love for Jamal, the last thing I would want to do is end what we have, but I can't fight religion, I can't fight politics, and I especially can not fight my father. I also do not want to take a chance at risking my life. With me being pregnant, once my family finds out, it seems like there is no great outcome whichever road I take. I have no choice, but to move back to Nigeria. But there is something that I do have a choice about. Tomorrow I am pleased to be meeting with a counselor at Planned Parenthood. Her job is to simply listen to me speak and she does not hold any bias opinions. Whether or not I choose to do it, the fact that I have a choice, the fact that I have a very low chance of morbidity/mortality, and the fact that Jamal is able to be right by my side through it all makes me feel truly safe and certain that whatever decision I make, I will be okay. I guess the best is yet to come after all.

The End

RHYMES WITH RYAN (On the Hill 2016)
by Cindy Cooper

ABOUT THE PLAY

CHARACTERS:
Paul Ryan: A member of the House of Representatives and its Speaker; especially exuberant about all things ultra conservative, whether or not they reflect reality
Jo-Jo: A junior staffer; may be male or female
Sally: A senior staffer, female

Setting: An office in the Longworth House Office Building, On the Hill, Washington, DC

Rhymes with Ryan (On the Hill 2016)

PAUL RYAN
(Sits in his office.)
Let's see. We have 1.1 trillion dollars in the federal budget, minus funds to those pesky clinics is ... let's see ... I need to figure this out ...

JO-JO
(JO-JO, a junior staffer, enters.)
Mr. Speaker. Sir. It's so early. Aren't you missing your morning workout?

PAUL RYAN
I'm doing up some important numbers. I'm a numbers guy, you know.

JO-JO
But, sir, we usually do that for you. Perhaps I can help.

PAUL RYAN
I'm looking for ways to save the federal budget.

JO-JO
Oh! I have some research on that! For example, we could save $628 billion dollars by ending loopholes for corporations. And by ending fossil fuel preferences, we could save $110 billion. And if we made one less drone ...

PAUL RYAN
What we need to do, we need to get rid of all these women's health clinics ... that that organization ... I can't even speak its name. The one that starts with the letters "PP."

JO-JO
Planned Parenthood?

PAUL RYAN
Yes ... that's the one!

SALLY
(SALLY, a senior staffer, enters.)
Mr. Speaker! Here you are. The Congressmen were looking for you at the gym! (beat) Mr. Speaker! You shaved your beard.

PAUL RYAN
Yes, yes I did. You know there are 300,000 hairs in a man's beard, and I shaved them all off.

JO-JO
300,000? That seems a little high. I'm sure I've read ...
(Looking it up quickly.)

SALLY
Shh! Mr. Ryan is the Speaker of the House and the Speaker is never wrong.

PAUL RYAN
It's true. I always get my numbers right.

JO-JO
Well, there was that tax return in 2011.

SALLY
You keep your voice down!

PAUL RYAN
I just forgot to report a little extra income. Ten years ago.

JO-JO
Five years ago. And it was fully one-fifth of your income.

SALLY
He amended it!
(to Ryan)
It doesn't matter, sir. Everyone knows you're a numbers guy, so it must have been an honest mistake.

JO-JO
Says here there are 7,000 hairs in the average beard.

PAUL RYAN
Well, 300,000 – 7,000 -- I wasn't far off. I probably have more, judging from all those marathons I've run.

JO-JO
One.

SALLY
Let's not go into that! The papers got it wrong.

JO-JO
He ran one marathon.

PAUL RYAN
My brother has run a bunch of marathons. I just confused my brother with me.

JO-JO
What ...?

SALLY
(Overlapping.)
An honest mistake. It could happen to anyone.

RYAN
And I was just rounding off when I said I ran it in three hours.

SALLY
You were definitely close.

JO-JO
Right. 4.1 hours can easily be rounded off to three.

SALLY
No matter. We're here to help YOU, Mr. Speaker. Mr. Ryan has a new idea to get rid of Planned Parenthood and all those other nasty independent clinics and women's centers, too! All at the same time. Isn't that exciting?

PAUL RYAN
Think how much we'll save in the budget!

JO-JO
Not really. All of the money that goes to the clinics combined wouldn't even come to 1-60th (one-sixtieth) of the cost of a single drone. If we cut one drone from the military budget ...

SALLY
We'll give that clinic money to CHURCHES!

JO-JO
But, people LIKE Planned Parenthood.

PAUL RYAN
See! That's the problem! People like these clinics. That's why we have to wipe them out.

SALLY
That's right. Those people are deviant. Only terrible people use them.

JO-JO
But you're talking about millions of people each year. And the clinics have very high favorability ratings. Higher than Congress. Higher than either party! And these are voters. I mean, my mother had a health scare ....

PAUL RYAN
See, there, kid ... you're pinpointing the problem. They vote!

SALLY
Exactly!

PAUL RYAN
What's worse -- THEY ENCOURAGE people to VOTE!

JO-JO
But don't we want people to vote? The purple finger and everything.

RYAN
We want OUR people to vote.

SALLY
Exactly! Not these deviant people.

PAUL RYAN
These people will never vote for us!

JO-JO
That's ... because you're trying to do away with the programs they support! My mother said ....

PAUL RYAN
We need to wipe them off the map.

SALLY
Like that Acorn group. Imagine -- they went door-to-door.
Registering people to vote! Any kind of people.

Oh oh! I know. We can have a fine for anybody who visits a
clinic! Retroactive!

PAUL RYAN
If they don't pay it, straight to the federal penitentiary!

JO-JO
But my mother just went to a clinic, and the people were
really nice.

RYAN
(blocks his ears and eyes)
I can't hear.

SALLY
(to Jo-Jo)
You be quiet if you want a job around here. You're upsetting the Speaker of the House.

JO-JO
I know my mother is just one person, but she had a matter
possibly related to ovarian cancer ...

PAUL RYAN
Is it over yet?

SALLY
(to Jo-Jo)
You -- get out!

JO-JO
Mom said there were all kinds of people at the clinic. Gay, trans, straight. Men ...

PAUL RYAN
Men? What men?

JO-JO
Men who need condoms. Or testing for sexually transmitted diseases ...

PAUL RYAN
Well, that's different if they serve men. How many men?

JO-JO
I don't know.

PAUL RYAN
Your mother's convinced me, kid! We will disband all the clinics but allow them to serve men. Manly men. Men who go hunting. Men who grow beards.

SALLY
Sir, I think that might be a problem. Gender discrimination laws, and all ...

PAUL RYAN
It's NOT a problem. I have the numbers! How many women are in the Declaration of Independence? None! That's right. Is there an Equal Rights Amendment? No! We took care of that! Sure, they slipped up ONE time in history and let women have the right to vote. But we're going to FIX that! This is a MAN'S country! This is a man's country! Come on, join me ...

SALLY
No... no. Sir. I mean ... women are ... people ...

JO-JO
(Simultaneously)
No ... WAY!

PAUL RYAN
Yeah! This ... is ... a ... MAN's COUNTRY! We've got it, we've
got it ....!

The End

SECTION FOUR: BODY POLITICS
Originally directed by Atonia Pettiford

On The Brink of Middle Age by Yvette Heyliger
The Goddess of Hygieia by Michael angel Johnson
Useless Uterus by Anne Flanagan
Chained Labor by Mildred Lewis
The Prisoner by Ellen Cohen

ON THE BRINK OF MIDDLE AGE
by Yvette Heyliger

ABOUT THE PLAY

"On the Brink of Middle Age" explores the mixed emotions of a woman entering a new stage of life and who, in a flash of insight, reclaims and redefines womanhood in the new millennium.

A solo work, it was performed by the writer at the Reproductive Freedom Festival

On the Brink of Middle Age

I am forty-nine today and I admit it: I am slowly losing my "friend."

My great-grandmother, my grandmother, my mother, all lost their "friends!" The Change of Life is a process that can spread over 13 years the doctor said. I don't know how to respond; what to think of this impending loss; how to handle being, *peri-menopausal.*

I see my daughters blossoming into womanhood a blossoming that started with: first steps, first words, first foods, first relaxers, bras, menstrual periods, "mother-daughter" talks, proms, high school and college graduations, first afros, gynecological visits, birth control, boyfriends—girlfriends—then boyfriends again, first engagement... what's left? Marriage, then... *grandchildren!*

Time is marching on. No longer blossoming, I am plucked—well plucked, in fact. I am all rusting pipes and mixed metaphors about getting older. Thank God, I am a woman of color. We hold up well. Comments from admirers bear this out: "Girl, you don't look like you have a daughter in college," or my favorite, "You two could be sisters!"

These statements hold some comfort for me, sure. But the truth is, I'm forty-nine and spreading, *and on the brink of what?* Saying goodbye to my monthly "friend" and hello too...

- Having hot flashes, night sweats and dizzy spells
- Adding invisible bifocals to my eye-glass prescription
- Dying persistent and increasingly grey hairs, black
- Getting three discrete tracks of hair sewn into my scalp to make up for the inevitable hair loss
- Propping up my sulking breasts in a padded bra
- Covering the "muffin top" that hangs over my belted pants with a loose fitting cotton shirt, or worse
- Stuffing myself into a girdle, hoping to recreate some semblance a waistline no longer there
- Wearing sensible shoes with orthotics
- Resurrecting some childhood trauma that I am told I am now old enough to handle emotionally
- Taking estrogen or calcium supplements
- *Wondering at what point a lubricant will become necessary for sex!*

I'm on the brink of a new stage of life. Lucky me! I used to be cute. I used to be charming. I used to be funny. I used to be skinny. That's right—had to wear men's jeans. You know why? No ass and no hips. And my breasts, like a Las Vegas show girl—each one could fill a champagne glass. I was *The Girl from Ipanema. (She sings.)* "Tall and tan and young and lovely, the girl from Ipanema goes walking..." I sunbathed nude on rooftops in Barcelona under the watchful eyes of orange-clad monks who should have been chanting.

I run to the long mirror in the hallway. I rip off my clothes and stand in front of it, looking at myself, *naked.* I turn around and look over my shoulder. I do have more junk in my trunk. I face forward... and under the hood too. I am my mother, and my mother's mother. I put on my robe and sit on the bed. It is true—I have let myself go. Thank goodness for my pretty skin, good teeth, formerly-beautiful-now-handsome-face, and winning personality.

I glance at the nightstand. The birthday bouquet which had greeted me that morning is annoyingly cheerful. I reach for the box of birthday chocolates and bewail the body I once had with each bite. I used to be a babe, a sweet young thing. Now I'm what—a cougar; ready to pounce on some unsuspecting, twenty-something-man-child to make myself feel young and attractive again?

I hear the key in the lock. My husband has come home early from work. He stands in the foyer rifling through the mail, grunting or sighing in response to each piece. He has been going through his own "male menopause" but he looks good to me. And he's only getting better with age; more handsome, and more distinguished, with that salt and pepper beard and miraculously full head of hair still. He's a middle-aged man in a young man's body. He's hot. And he knows it. And I know it too, so I decide to confront him. He looks up from the sorted mail, surprised.

"Honey, why aren't you dressed? We have dinner reserva—"

"Why did you buy me these chocolates?"

"What do you mean? It's your birthday. I always buy you—"

"Yea and why is that? Are you trying to fatten me up so you can have an excuse? Twenty years and two kids—it's about that time isn't it?" I cut him off before he can respond. "Don't deny it, just tell me now, and tell me fast!" (I think that if he tells me fast, it won't hurt so much—sort of like ripping off a Band-Aid, you have to do it fast.) "Are you going to leave me for a younger woman, because... I would rather **die**, than be a cliché!" I brace myself for his answer. Suddenly, I am more *naked* now than I was when I stood before the mirror.

He rests the sorted mail on the table and says, "I don't want a younger woman. I just want you fit, and strong, and healthy, so we can grow old together."

I am silent. And then I realize all is not lost. I don't have a foot in the grave just yet. "Fit, and strong, and healthy..." I can do that! Why, just the other day the talking head on the evening news declared: "Thirty is the new twenty and forty is the new thirty." I postpone the dinner reservation, give my black man a snack, and go out for a power walk. *There's no reason fifty can't be the new forty!*

The End

THE GODDESS OF HYGIEIA
by Michael angel Johnson

ABOUT THE PLAY

Inspired by the lives of Harriot Kezia Hunt (1805-1875) and Edmonia Wildfire Lewis (C.1843-1907).

Characters:

Harriot Kezia Hung (Dr. Hunt): Caucasian, around 57

98

Edmonia Wildfire Lewis: The first woman of African-American and Chippewa Indian descent to earn an international reputation as a visual artist, around 19

Setting:

It is around 1862
Boston, Massachusetts
32 Green Street

The Goddess of Hygieia

The sun is beginning to set, so the light in the waiting room is a golden hue. The sign on the door reads: "Ladies Physiological Society of Boston." DR. HUNT is at the door. The sound of CHILDREN playing can be heard. DR. HUNT hands the WOMAN on the other side of the door a container.

DR. HUNT
(Referring to the contents of the container)
Give the children this first thing in the morning and before they go to bed at night and make sure you take some yourself. Pneumonia is serious. And wash each glass, dish, plate, silverware, and pot the way I showed you. Miss Lewis, what a surprise, come in.

EDMONIA LEWIS, limping, enters the clinic. DR. HUNT continues to speak to the WOMAN on the other side of the door. MISS LEWIS paces nervously.

You and the children need to come back to see me next week...make it Wednesday.

DR. HUNT closes the door and then turns to MISS LEWIS.

The spread of diseases and sometimes the disease itself can be prevented by good hygiene. Now, what can I do for you?

MISS LEWIS
I was in the neighborhood, Dr. Hunt...and when you came to my studio with Mrs. Shaw...you talked about your clinic...how you were helping the mothers and children of Boston...

DR. HUNT
So you've come about your leg...

MISS LEWIS
What?

DR. HUNT
You're limping more than you did at your studio. Pull your skirt up?

MISS LEWIS
Excuse me?

DR. HUNT
I need to examine your leg.

MISS LEWIS pulls up her skirt.

There's some swelling.

DR. HUNT goes to a cabinet where there are many herbs.

MISS LEWIS
What's all that?

DR. HUNT
Herbs. I shall make up a mixture for the swelling.

MISS LEWIS
You don't bleed your patients?

DR. HUNT
Most of the male doctors do, but I don't. On a scale from one to ten where would you place the pain?

MISS LEWIS
(Choosing a random number)
Ten.

DR. HUNT
To be in such pain, you are very calm...

MISS LEWIS
I meant to say six. Doctors make me nervous...even though I don't like it, bleeding...

DR. HUNT
Does not offer balance...

MISS LEWIS
"Balance"?

DR. HUNT
To heal the body, all aspects of the body must come together to create balance, and bleeding does not do that. Now, is the pain in one place or all through the leg?

MISS LEWIS
All through. You left my studio before we could talk...

DR. HUNT
About what? Oh, you mean your leg....

MISS LEWIS
I meant about my sculptures....

DR. HUNT
Is it a shooting pain when it comes or...?

MISS LEWIS
Shooting. Mrs. Shaw has commissioned me to do a sculpture of her son....

DR. HUNT
Mrs. Shaw is putting on a brave face, having her son fighting in this war is taking a toll on her nerves...

MISS LEWIS
Colonel Shaw is leading the first all-black regiment to fight in the Civil War...

DR. HUNT
Mrs. Shaw may be an abolitionist, but she's still a Mother, who is worried about her son. I want to take a look at your left foot.

MISS LEWIS
Why?

DR. HUNT
You suffered a bad break on your right leg, which can cause problems when depending too much on the left foot to walk. When did you break...?

MISS LEWIS
A year ago.

DR. HUNT
Weren't you student at Oberlin College at that time...?

MISS LEWIS
My left foot is fine....

Despite the protest, DR. HUNT unlaces MISS LEWIS' shoe.

DR. HUNT
It's important to take care of yourself, Miss Lewis. Women refuse to understand that...they try to help everyone else...

MISS LEWIS
I'm not some charity case like that woman and her children you were speaking with when I came in...

DR. HUNT
I'm merely informing you about how you are depending too much on the left foot...

DR. HUNT takes MISS LEWIS' shoe off.

And there's bruising on the foot...

MISS LEWIS
Where did you study medicine, and you talk about this balance...

DR. HUNT
Are you implying that I don't know what I'm doing...?

MISS LEWIS
I heard Mrs. Shaw and some of the other abolitionists talking about....

DR. HUNT
Oh, they enjoy telling my story when it's really not theirs to tell....

MISS LEWS
To be the first woman rejected from Harvard Medical School is not really a badge of courage, is it?

DR. HUNT
But I did apply, gain, in 1850 and I was accepted. And now that we've discussed my history, let's move on. I'm going to give you a salve to use at night on your left foot...

DR. HUNT begins making up the salve.

MISS LEWIS
I really didn't mean to...it's just that my leg does hurt. Maybe not a 10, but it does hurt....
(Silence)
There were so many people at my studio the other day that I didn't have a chance to, personally, show you around.... You must come again, so I can...

DR. HUNT
I don't have time; this clinic keeps me busy....I was merely accompanying Mrs. Shaw...

MISS LEWIS
How would you like it if I said Oh, I really didn't come here because you are this wonderful doctor, but I just happened to be in the neighborhood....

DR. HUNT
But why else would you come here?

MISS LEWIS
My point is that you take pride in what you do, and I, also, take pride in my work...

DR. HUNT
That leg really didn't heal well. How did you break...?

MISS LEWIS
My leg is not the point. I want to talk about something that Mrs. Shaw mentioned about you....

DR. HUNT
Everybody knows. It's not something I want to discuss.

MISS LEWIS
Of course, it can be upsetting to think about the end of....

DR. HUNT
I'll give you the salve and then you may leave.

MISS LEWIS
What happened to you at Harvard Medical...?

DR. HUNT
I'm sure they told you. And it doesn't really concern...

MISS LEWIS
Someone like me, is that why you didn't look at my sculptures? You don't think a woman of my color...

DR. HUNT
Don't be ridiculous—

MISS LEWIS
Then why don't you want to talk to me about...?

DR. HUNT
At Harvard, I was harassed so much by male students that it was impossible for me to attend classes. I'm not proud of that fact. I don't enjoy talking about....

MISS LEWIS
I was physical attacked at Oberlin and that's how my leg was broken. And I don't like talking...

DR. HUNT
It seems that education does come at a high price for some of us. And to be clear, I did look at your sculptures. Here's the salve.

DR. HUNT hands Miss Lewis the salve.

MISS LEWIS
How much for..?

DR. HUNT
Ten cents.

MISS LEWIS takes the money out of her purse.

MISS LEWIS
And what did you think of my work?

DR. HUNT
As you well know, and, as the people of Boston are saying, you're talented. Now, I have house calls to make. You can put your shoe on and see yourself out...

MISS LEWIS
(Begins the lace up her shoe.)
So, how did you finally become a doctor?

DR. HUNT
This couple, Mr. and Mrs. Smith from England, saved my sister's life when she had tuberculosis. I studied with them, and they taught me about herbs, which is a much better form of medicine.

MISS LEWIS
And I left Oberlin after the attack and came to Boston and discovered sculpting.

DR. HUNT
Well, it seems we both have accomplished what we wanted. Have a good evening, Miss Lewis....

MISS LEWIS
Mrs. Shaw told me that you want to commission a sculptor to create a work of art for your gravesite at Mt. Auburn Cemetery. Let me create the piece.

DR. HUNT
Your work is good, but I don't think you...

MISS LEWIS
Harvard at first didn't think you were good enough...

DR. HUNT
This is different...this is very personal....This statute will identify me for all eternity...It will be my legacy...

MISS LEWIS
Hygieia.

DR.HUNT
What?

MISS LEWIS
Hygieia is the goddess of hygiene. Isn't that the beginning of this "balance" that you believe in? Isn't that what you're teaching the women and children here? Who better to represent you for eternity, Dr. Hunt, than the goddess Hygieia?

Blackout

USELESS UTERUS
by Anne Flanagan

ABOUT THE PLAY

CHARACTERS:
Mary – a patient
Doctor – her OB/GYN
Off stage voice

Useless Uterus

Lights up. Mary is in her OB/GYN's office. The DOCTOR stands, showing her an X-ray.

DOCTOR
You see, this is an X Ray of a normal uterus. And this, Mary, is yours.

MARY
It's huge!

DOCTOR
Yes. Your uterus is severely enlarged. That's that clock you hear ticking.

MARY
I don't hear a -

DOCTOR
It's not your fault. It's biological. Your uterus is barren, empty - begging to be filled.

MARY
Okay, well, I plan to have children.

DOCTOR
But you haven't! You must heed the Call of Nature.

MARY
I will someday -

DOCTOR
Someday?! Look here, Woman! You've run out of time. That uterus of yours must be filled - or it will explode!

MARY
Explode?!

DOCTOR
Ka-POW!

MARY
Is that really a thing? I've never heard that - I didn't know!

DOCTOR
Because the Government doesn't want you to.

MARY
But, I'm not even dating.

DOCTOR
There are options.

MARY
Like sperm banks? Donor eggs?

DOCTOR
Mmmm - I'm thinking outside the box.

MARY
Invitro?

DOCTOR
Nooo - I'm thinking candy.

MARY
I - what?

DOCTOR
Candy. Sugary confections, usually bite sized.

MARY
Yes, but what does candy have to do with -

DOCTOR
Instead of a candy dish, many women opt to store their sweets in their -

MARY
Are you on crack?!

DOCTOR
Of course not. I only take safe drugs. Like OxyContin. If you don't like candy, there is another, more proactive approach. It's really quite brilliant.

MARY
Okaaay -

DOCTOR
Toxic waste.

MARY
Excuse me?!

DOCTOR
The government has run out of dumping sites and with that uterus of yours, you could store a ton!

MARY
You're insane!

DOCTOR
They pay a sizeable rental fee.

MARY
I am NOT storing toxic waste in my body!

DOCTOR
Well, you must use that uterus for something, otherwise, why were you put on this earth?

MARY
Are you saying women are only good for -

DOCTOR
Plus you are willfully endangering your health! As your physician, I have a duty to protect your well being. And as a man, I have a duty to dictate what you do with your reproductive organs.

MARY
That is such bull-

DOCTOR
As such, I've taken the liberty of signing you up for another option.

MARY
You signed up me?

DOCTOR
Yup! This one's win/win - it enables both of us to 'give back' if you will.

MARY
Surrogacy?

DOCTOR
In a way, yes, it is a form of housing. You see, Mary, we medical professionals have inked a deal with the penitentiary system. To alleviate prison overcrowding.

MARY
I don't unders-

DOCTOR
For the next five to ten years, your uterus will house two drunk drivers, a bank robber and a drug dealing Neo Nazi!

OFF STAGE VOICE
SIG HEIL!

MARY
HAVE YOU LOST YOUR FREAKING MIND?!

DOCTOR
No need to thank me, Sugar tits - just doing my job.

Mary attempts to run but the Doctor pins her down.

(calling) Recess is over, boys! Back to your cells!

MARY
NOOOOO!

End of Play

CHAINED LABOR
by Mildred Inez Lewis

ABOUT THE PLAY

TIME: Evening, Now

SETTING: Bronx Apartment

CHARACTERS
Willow – 39, African American
Attallah – 22, Willow's daughter
Ebony – 24, Willow's daughter

Chained Labor

Single mother WILLOW (39, African American) paces in her spotless, hard won Bronx living room. She squirts some cleaning fluid into the air, sighs in the smell, then resumes pacing.

ATTALLAH (O.S.)
Ma!

WILLOW
Here.

She relaxes and sits.

Her daughters, EBONY (24) and ATTALLAH (22) enter. They're back from an anti-police brutality protest, t-shirts in hand.

EBONY
We snagged you two.

ATTALLAH
One for the gym and another for around the house.

WILLOW
That's all right. You keep them.

ATTALLAH
They said there were 1,000 people there, but it was at least double that.

WILLOW
Good. More people, more problems.

EBONY
Ma. You were worried.

WILLOW
Can't help it.

EBONY
You know we're careful.

WILLOW
That doesn't mean a thing.

ATTALLAH
Okay, let's go to the happy place. Focus on the shirts. They're better than the last ones.

EBONY
They're real quality. More like Sean John than Roca. Try one on.

WILLOW
Not now.

EBONY
You should've come with us.

WILLOW
I told you, no.

ATTALLAH
Sorry.

WILLOW
It's too sad for me. I won't go there.

EBONY
If we don't fight, how do things get better? Things have got to change.

WILLOW
For who? We're doing all right.

ATTALLAH
Our people. We have an obligation.

WILLOW
You don't get that mess from me.

EBONY
Mom!

WILLOW
Let's get on to something else.

EBONY
It felt good to be back in the old neighborhood. We marched past St. Bart's.

Willow doesn't respond.

ATTALLAH
Where we were born?

Willow squeezes Attallah's hand.

WILLOW
Only good memory from that place is you.

EBONY
What about me?

WILLOW
You know I meant both of you.

EBONY
It's not what you said.

ATTALLAH
(to EBONY)
Can you stop trying to make a federal case out of everything?

EBONY
Aren't I a good memory too, ma?

WILLOW
It's different.

EBONY
Why?

WILLOW
It just is.

ATTALLAH
(to EBONY)
She works her butt off for us. Leave it alone.

EBONY
What is it mom? Because I'm darker?

ATTALLAH
You know she's not like that.

EBONY
Because her dad at least tried to pay child support? Maybe I remind you too much –

Willow slaps her.

WILLOW
I shouldn't have done that.

EBONY
At least you're angry. At least you feel something.

WILLOW
You're a different generation. We just took it. I don't know what to make of you sometimes.

ATTALLAH
We need older people to stop looking the other way. They let that boy bleed out on the street.

WILLOW
Don't you think I felt every hour of that boy's life slipping away?

EBONY
I don't know what you feel. Just that we never seem to be good no matter what I do.

WILLOW
How can you say that?

Ebony tears up.

WILLOW
I should've told you this long ago.

EBONY
Told me what?

WILLOW
(to ATTALLAH)
Maybe you should step out for a second.

EBONY
I want her to hear it.

WILLOW
(steadies herself)
Okay, okay. You know I used to use. That I had some trouble with the law.

ATTALLAH
That's all in the past. Ma, you've always been open with us.

WILLOW
No. Ebony, I was locked up until you were three months old.

EBONY
Where was I?

WILLOW
For the first two days you were with me.

EBONY
Just two days?

WILLOW
I loved on you so hard. I fought to keep you.

EBONY
Why didn't you tell me?

WILLOW
There's more to it.

EBONY
What?

WILLOW
The stress and the drugs, the way I was living, I was high risk. When your time came, I begged. I didn't want you born in a jail infirmary. Maybe it's why you're so angry.

EBONY
I'm not angry. I'm hurt.

WILLOW
I didn't have violent priors, only drugs. I never tried to run. But as soon as we got to St. Bart's, they shackled me. They only left one leg free.

ATTALLAH
Were you in pain? That was stupid. Sorry.

WILLOW
I couldn't turn without hurting my wrist. They left me un-covered. Here I was 19, your dad in the service. He was the only one who'd ever seen me naked and I was chained to a table with my coochie out for everyone to see. Nurses, aides, doctors. All the hustle bustle of a hospital.

By the time the second baby comes along, you open your legs for anybody. But then ... The guards sat in the back. I was so shamed. Since they acted like I was a murderer, I didn't even ask to use the restroom. I went on the table.

EBONY
Ma ...

WILLOW
Let me finish. It was a lady doctor. I'll never forget her. She finally got them to take off the handcuffs because I couldn't help push. They took off one. I wanted to hold onto your face and look at you, but with one hand I couldn't support your head, then there was no time. They kept me chained all the way through to recovery.

Ebony and Attallah hug her.

WILLOW
My love for you both is so ...

She gestures its vastness.

So when you march and write letters that I don't all the way understand, I'm afraid. But I know you're not doing it for whatever "them," you're doing it for me, too.

EBONY AND ATTALAH
Us.

They embrace each other.

The End

THE PRISONER
by Ellen Cohen

ABOUT THE PLAY

Adapted from *Laboring: Stories of a New York City Hospital Midwife* by the author, a Certified Nurse Midwife

The prisoner

Lincoln Hospital in the South Bronx is the unadorned red brick building that looms over the railroad tracks as commuter trains from Grand Central and Penn Station cross the Harlem River from Manhattan to the Bronx. I worked here as a midwife from 1983, fresh out of school, until 1990. During those years I cared for thousands of pregnant women and girls, and delivered some 800 babies. This is the story of a birth I will never forget...

A policeman stationed outside the Labor and Delivery examination room meant that the patient awaiting my care was a prisoner. Perhaps she had been brought to Lincoln from the huge complex of court buildings near Yankee Stadium, not far from the hospital, or the nearby 40th police precinct.

The woman was moaning softly to herself as I entered the room. She seemed to be in active labor. But before I could introduce myself, ask about her health history and do a physical exam, the sight of handcuffs shackling her to the gurney made me stop short.

Although trembling inside – outrage mingled with fear that my intervention might be useless -- I summoned my most authoritative "doctor" voice to address her guard.

"Uncuff the patient," I told him. "I can't take care of her like this – it's not safe." To soften the request I added, "She won't go anywhere, believe me." Out came the officer's keys and the cuffs disappeared without the fight I had feared. But instead of feeling relieved at successfully advocating for humane treatment for my patient, I felt mortified. Witnessing the humiliation the woman suffered made it hard for me to even look at her, even though I was not the one inflicting such cruelty. Her shame became mine.

With one now-freed hand the patient rubbed her belly, clutching my arm with the other. Soon afterward I helped her give birth to a healthy son. She got to hold her newborn for a few minutes before being shackled again. I don't know what happened to either mother or baby after that.
Stories like this rarely have happy endings.

I thought about this patient in August, 2009, when New York's then-Governor David Paterson signed legislation outlawing the shackling of women prisoners during childbirth in this state. But despite a decades-long campaign by the Legal Aid Society, National Advocates for

Pregnant Women and others to end such brutal treatment, pregnant and laboring prisoners all over the U.S. still endure being chained like animals during birth.

The End

A CHANGE OF HEART, SO TO SPEAK
by Kitty Chen

ABOUT THE PLAY

The play is a short metaphoricopsychoanatomical farce in which a woman undergoes transplant for a overly caring heart and loses more than she bargained for. This version is excerpted from a longer work.

Cast:
SURGEON - any age over 30
WOMAN - late 30s
(ANESTHESIOLOGIST – Off stage voice)

NOTE: The play needs a light playful touch. Yes, it's excessive, absurd, over-the-top, and just plain silly. However, it is based on deep-seated feelings (ie, terror) about our bodies and the medical system that attends to them.

Forced heavy manic/hysterical acting will kill the play. Light manic/hysterical acting and playful excessiveness are vital. The actors must be verbal and facile, be able to drive the play, and play the farce and absurdity while having full understanding of the underlying desperation and irrational fears.

It needs to go very fast.

A Change of Heart, So To Speak

Surgeon's examining room. Patient, a proper suburban lady in her late 30s, appears to have been waiting for hours but contains her desperation. Surgeon, any age over 30, enters without looking at her and heads straight for her chart, on desk.

SURGEON
So, young lady, what seems to be the problem?

PATIENT
It-it's my heart.

SURGEON
Nonsense--you're still fairly young, you're not obese. Besides, you're a woman! It says so right here.

PATIENT
No no no! I mean, yes I am but that's not what I mean....oh dear, you'll think I'm being silly.

SURGEON
I can decide that for myself, if you don't mind.

PATIENT
Please forgive me. The problem is...I c-c-care too much.

SURGEON
Care?

PATIENT
I c-c-c-care too much.

SURGEON
Could you be more precise? Do you mean care as in care package?

PATIENT
Don't get me wrong--I send care packages to everybody I know--I know I should send them to people I don't know too. But it's those little styrofoam peanuts--they STICK to me! I JUST CAN'T STAND IT!

SURGEON
Quiet! Do you mean "care", as in care-taker? Answer briefly.

PATIENT
I take care of everything there is to be taken care of--god knows no one else will. I'm talking about something more... more...

SURGEON
Emotional?

PATIENT
That's it! I have emotional pain in my heart. All the time.

SURGEON
Wonderful! Madame, you've come to the right place. I am the best surgeon in the township for Pain Due to Emotions! Best supply of hearts in the whole county. Anesthesiologist right next door. Medals of honor, countless commendations. Tell me all about it.

PATIENT
I care too much about everybody! I feel so responsible for everything!

SURGEON
Please describe the clinical signs and symptoms.

PATIENT
I apologize to every homeless person I see. Is that a clinical sign and symptom?

SURGEON
Go on.

PATIENT
I want to embrace them, give them all my money, why do they run away from me?

SURGEON
Could be your approach. Go on.

PATIENT
Sarajevo! Ohhh, how I weep for you! I want to stand in the line of fire and cry out: "You bully Serbs just leave those poor Bosnians and Herzegovinians alone!"

SURGEON
That's quite a mouthful. You're responsible for them too?

PATIENT
Of course. But the pain is worst when anything happens to my Little Danny. And Little Danny Jr. Last week I was rushing to work and I gave Little Danny Jr cold dry cereal--out of the box!--instead of steaming-hot wholesome whole-grain oatmeal!

SURGEON
Tsk tsk tsk.

PATIENT
That very same day he fell on the playground and skinned his sweet little knee.

She falls to the ground, wailing uncontrollably.

I did it! It was all my fault!

SURGEON
Madame. Get up please. Without a doubt you have a case of Women Who Care Far Too Much About Everybody and Feel Absurdly Responsible for Everything No Matter How Far Removed From Their Sphere of Influence. Nothing to worry about. All women suffer from this disease at one time or another. Your case is simply more advanced. Happily for you, I have a new definitive cure.

PATIENT
Oh doctor! You've given me back my life.

SURGEON
We simply remove your old heart and give you a nice new one. A change of heart, so to speak. Guaranteed no more heartache. (smiling) Would you like a hysterectomy while we're at it?

PATIENT
No thank you. Little Danny and I plan to have a baby girl as soon as we can. Before it's too late, if you know what I mean.

SURGEON
I can fit you in...how about right now?

PATIENT
Now? H-H-Here?

SURGEON
It's a routine office procedure. Is there some problem?

PATIENT
I'm sure it's silly of me. I-I just feel I need a little t-t-time.

SURGEON
(terminating the interview)
Well! If that's the way you feel--

PATIENT
No no no no! I'll do anything you say!

SURGEON
Fine, then we're all set. Why don't you make yourself comfortable on that table over there while I get everything ready. Go on now.

Patient fearfully, and with a trace of growing resentment, lies down, pulls sheet over herself. Surgeon puts on surgical gown and gloves.

PATIENT
Shouldn't a scrub nurse be doing that for you? Sir. *(his putting on gloves)* Like on TV?

SURGEON
What's it take to scrub? Look I'm worn out!--I did 22 hysterectomies this morning!

PATIENT
I didn't realize.

She watches surgeon warily.

Er...are you going to put me to sleep sometime soon?

SURGEON
Oh! Right! Anesthesiologist! Get the hell in here you!

PATIENT
Er, just one more little question?

SURGEON
(snarling)
Why don't you just sue me for malpractice?

PATIENT
My new heart. I'd like to...see it?

SURGEON
Picky picky picky!

He takes out a great big heart.

It's heavy duty. Hope it won't keep you from having a good time.

PATIENT
(consternation)
Isn't it a little...immense?

SURGEON
It'll last you a good long time! Now lie down and no more nonsense! Where is that stupid anesthesiologist? Oh damn, it's Friday golf! No problem. I love administering the sleepy time.

As Surgeon prepares the syringe, he is drawn to staring at her abdomen as if mesmerized.

My! what a nice round abdomen you have!

Patient
NO! Up here! It's the heart! You're doing my heart!

SURGEON
Oh Right, right!

He gives patient a shot. She is out.

Finally some peace and quiet. Now I can practice my art.

He makes big incision, opens flaps. He tries to shove in the heart, but it's too big.

Couldn't they have found a better fit?
It's the Wrong Heart! This is a Caring Heart--to cure Callous People Who Couldn't Care Less! It's supposed to be a Callous Heart--forWomenWhoCareFarTooMuchAboutEverythingAndFeel AbsurdlyResponsiEtcEtc! Someone must have misfiled it!

She starts to stir.

Oh no! She's coming to!

He knocks her over the head with a blunt instrument.

She'll never know the difference. I'll send her for some psychiatry afterwards.

He tosses aside viscera left and right, hums merrily.

Ahh, now there's plenty of room. What's this? A lump! It looks malignant. Should I...? I must! It would be unconscionable to leave it. --"Above all, do no harm!"

He removes and tosses aside more viscera, humming.

Such nice work. I hope she appreciates my improvisatory flair.

Patient starts to stir and moan.

Not yet--not yet!

He quickly stitches her up.

Okay, you can wake up now.

PATIENT
Am I different?
(jumps up to "try out" her new heart.)

SURGEON
I did a brilliant job against formidable odds. Oh I'm so exhausted.

PATIENT
I think I feel different. Yes! I do! I feel like...like a lioness in the wild!

SURGEON
Good day, madame. *(hands her a bill, shouts offstage)* Next!

PATIENT
(reads bill)
"Heart transplant, 1 million smackers." Oh well, it's worth it...."Bilateral total mastectomy"???

SURGEON
It's all right, there's no charge. See? NC--no charge.

PATIENT
WHY DID YOU GIVE ME A MASTECTOMY!

SURGEON
Calm down! I found a little lump--there in your left breast. You should be grateful!

PATIENT
A little lump?

SURGEON
It looked malignant!

PATIENT
My left breast?

SURGEON
Yes! Whatever!

PATIENT
WHY THE HELL DID YOU TAKE THEM BOTH OFF??

SURGEON
Laaadddy! CANCER! GROWS!

The End

PAPYRUS
by Laura Shamas

ABOUT THE PLAY

Cast Size: 2 women, Dr. A. & Dr. B.

Time: Now.

Papyrus

Lights up on: Two women in a museum office, wearing white jackets, special gloves and masks, examine an ancient papyrus roll. There's a magnifying glass nearby.

DR. A.
Unbelievable! Amazing!

DR. B.
Are you sure?
DR. A. tasks off her mask, looks at it again with the magnifying glass.

DR. A.
Yes. I think it is. I really think it is.

DR. B.
I need to brush up on my Middle Kingdom hieroglyphics to
be certain. But at first glance --

DR. A.
(Peering)
Oh, I can read it. It's hieratic, not hieroglyphic. It's part of
the oldest set of birth control instructions on the planet. I'd
swear it is. Good find, Brenda! Well done!

DR. B takes off her mask.

DR. B.
Thank you. It was just rolled up next to one of the old Helleniistic urns down there on Basement Level 4, where it's
quite dark and creepy.

DR. A.
Could it be an additional fragment linked to the famous
Kahun Gynaecological Papyrus? Or perhaps the Ebers Papyrus? Or perhaps another medical document never before
discovered -- it's all so exciting!

DR. B.
(Shrugs)
You know, I'm not really an Egyptologist. Per se. My area is
Medieval Chirography--

DR. A.
Well, this papyrus has birth control instructions. Just like the Ebers papyrus, if I recall. The Ebers papyrus is from Luxor around 1850 B.C.E., but its information is considered even older, perhaps thousands of years older, handed down orally until recorded--

DR. B.
So even four or five thousand years ago, women were concerned with birth control. What does it say? Can you translate a formula?

DR. A
(Peering with magnifying glass)
Here's a remedy. "Mash up... a bunch of dates, fresh honey and an herb"...not sure..."acacia? Then... Apply to cloth. Insert to vagina. Proceed."

DR. B.
That's quite sticky.

DR. A.
(Shrugs)
Sounds more like dessert than birth control. Those ancient Egyptians.

DR. B.
They knew how to live. What's another one?

DR. A.
(Reading again)
"To prevent pregnancy, cut up crocodile dung, and sprinkle where needed."

DR. B.
Just the very smell of crocodile dung alone would have an effect on the act--

DR. A.
(Puts down magnifying glass)
Right. Well, let's roll it up. Carefully now.

DR. B.
Right.

They roll it up together.

DR. A.
(Holding the rolled papyrus)
Brenda, this very papyrus could be the Da Vinci Code of Birth Control Papyri. We may have found the oldest birth control remedy manual in existence. I mean, you. You may have found it.

DR. B.
Of course. Yes, I found it. But the museum owns it. And we're already on the security camera.

She waves, indicating above them.

Hi, Security Camera.

DR. A.
Of course. So we'll put it in the safe. We'll get it verified. But you can release a book about it. I'll translate the papyrus. The museum can exhibit it. It's a win/win.

DR. B.
Great. What's our title? I'll try. "Dates and Dung and How It's Done." Or: "From Papyrus to Pap Smear."

DR. A.
Either one. And the subtitle: "How We've Always Cared About Birth Control."

They shake hands. Blackout.

The End

MID LIFE CHOICE
by Jessica Feder-Birnbaum

ABOUT THE PLAY:

A Monologue

Mid Life Choice

It's that time of the month. But the tampon wrappers are not in the bathroom wastebasket. Your cycle must be irregular since you turned 40. The cat jumps on your stomach. She did that the last two times. How could this happen? You used protection. You run out and buy a home pregnancy test. Just in case. You read the directions and proceed. You wait a few minutes. The line turns pink.

Your husband is sitting at the desk in the foyer of your apartment. He's starting a new business and is surrounded by boxes. He looks terrified when you show him the stick with the pink line.

You don't and you do think twice. Your kids are older – nine and seven. They share a bedroom. You gave away the stroller and the changing table. Where would a baby go? You find an abortion clinic in the yellow pages. You make an appointment for that afternoon. You have never questioned any other woman's decision, no matter how far along. You think about friends from high school. Horrific stories in the news – other moms. You are vehemently pro choice. But you've never had to terminate a pregnancy. You google Jewish law and talk to your husband. He says you can keep it.

The choice has to be yours. You tell him you won't get rid of it, if there's a heartbeat.

The clinic is in a nondescript office building. There are no signs advertising its presence. Still, menacing protestors stand on the sidewalk holding posters with photos of maimed fetuses. Your husband grabs your hand and you enter the lobby.

The reception area feels dour with its mauve vinyl chairs and industrial carpet. The place is packed. A gray haired woman has tears in her eyes. She can't have another baby. She's a grandmother, she explains. No one looks happy.

You fill out paperwork before you meet with a counselor. Your husband waits. You tell her the date of your last period. You're told that you have options. If you're pregnant, you can keep the baby. A nurse draws blood and a doctor examines your cervix. They determine that you're about five weeks along. The embryo hasn't taken shape. It's the size of a thumbnail. They take a sonogram. There is no heartbeat. You are told to make an appointment for the following week. You are adamant that the procedure gets done immediately. You schedule it for the next day.

It's early Saturday morning – a crisp October day. You go alone, so your husband can watch the kids. The protestors are holding their signs. They stare at you with hatred and cry out murderer! You hang your head and slip past.

When you get upstairs you give your insurance card to the receptionist.

You change into a hospital gown and are led to a backroom. It feels like a factory. Multiple examination beds are separated by partitions. Several women are having abortions done at the same time. There are moans of agony. You are given anesthesia and spread your legs. The doctor takes out a suction device, and you drift off. When you wake up, the doctor tells you that everything went fine although you were almost too early in the pregnancy to have this done. You shake your head. Had you waited any longer you couldn't have gone through with it. The anesthesia wears off and you're doubled over in pain. You're told to expect severe cramps and bleeding. Plan to go home and rest for the remainder of the day.

You barely remember making a follow up appointment. When you exit walking stiffly, the right-to-lifers are still there. They shake their fists. You evil baby killer, they shout. Invisible knives sear through your abdomen. You gasp for air.

The apartment is empty. You take two Advil and crawl into bed. Your body curled in a fetal position. You breathe through cramps and search for solace. Neighbors won't knock on your door with casseroles. There will be no baby naming or bris. Tears flow into an ocean of sadness. You grieve for what might have been. As the sobs cease, there is a wave of relief. You made a difficult choice. But it was yours to make. And for you it was the right decision.

The End

THE LAST REFUGE
by Henry Howard

ABOUT THE PLAY

A poem, "The Last Refuge" was presented by three performers at the Reproductive Freedom Festival.

The Last Refuge

By ones and twos,
By car or train, or on tired feet,
The women of Mississippi
Make their way to the last refuge
Of the Jackson Women's Health Organization.

Some come shyly,
With awkward partners,
And with trembling hands complete the forms
Acknowledging their new reality
As unintended parents.

Others come with women friends,
Seeking the solidarity of sisterhood
In the hardest decision to challenge
Already complicated lives.

And a few come strongly, defiantly,
Comfortable with the rightness of their choice,
Fierce in their determination
That choice belongs to them and must be fought for.

The clinic defenders come,
Women and men linking arms
And, with arms outstretched,
Embracing the hope of a bold new day
When no one rules and everyone chooses,
And gender equality is a simple sentence
Under the law.

And the antis gather, too,
With their hate-filled chants
And their fear-filled posters,
And their fervent belief
That forced motherhood
Is God's law, and men were decreed
To impose it.

Sooner or later,
No matter their differences
And different agendas,
Everyone comes to Jackson,
To the last refuge on the quiet street
Where actions speak louder than words,

Actions to keep reproductive choice alive
And keep women alive,
Even as the actions of a woman-hating Governor,
Lips oozing words of interjection and interference,
And misogynist nullification,
Threaten to wage war on women
For the sake of the unborn.

The women who come here seeking help
Must travel the length and breadth of Mississippi,
A journey of hours
For a medical procedure of mere minutes.

The doctors who care about women's health
Must fly for hours from other states,
And don a bullet-proof vest
Beneath their favorite workshirt.

Many people dress for success.
Abortion providers must dress
Simply to survive.

Yes, everyone comes to Jackson,
And what happens in Jackson
Stays in Jackson,
Including the last pink house
That stands like a public rock
Between women
And their private hell.

Neither Mississippi twister
Nor twisted laws
Can tear down the walls
Of the bright pink house!

Even as the courts and the Governor
Self-righteously proclaim,
"This clinic is closed!"
We must shout from the rooftops and the streets,
With all our might and for as long as it takes,
"This clinic stays open!"

The End

SECTION SIX: WHAT WE KNOW
Originally directed by Melanie Sutherland

Ida Mae Murphy by Debbie Miller
Ain't I A Woman by Nicole Goodwin
Sister by Mercedes Sanchez
Spare Rib (excerpts from a play) by Winter Miller
Blessed (excerpts) by Alix Olson

IDA MAE MURPHY
by Debbie L. Miller

ABOUT THE PLAY

A Monologue.

Ida Mae Murphy, 28, is sitting in Mosquito Alley, a roadside diner on the Alaska Highway, just outside Fairbanks, Alaska, 1959, the year of Alaska statehood.

Ida Mae Murphy

I'm from Arkansas. Riley's Holler, to be exact. It ain't New York, but it's where I'm from.

Let's talk about what's really important. The light is important. It's how we see life—how we perceive ourselves in relation to the universe, how we picture the world we dream about, discover who we are. It's all about the light. Sometimes, it's shinin' bright; other times, it's soft and subdued. But, it's always revealin.' And, the light here in Alaska is fantastic.

Some folks don't think I got much sense, 'cuz I'm a beautician. But, I'm an artist, and fixing folks' hair so they look their best is an art. Sometimes, I get a customer, and I'll talk to her and find out what's important to her and then I try to express the light through her hair. And, in that way, I communicate my art.

Lucy and Ethel understand. Lucy and Ethel are my cats. Lucy's a calico, and Ethel's a tabby. The night before I left for this here Alaska trip, I sat 'em down and explained to 'em that Momma was gonna be away for a little while, but that she'd think about 'em every day. I could tell by the way they was purrin', that they approved.

Now, when I heard about this caravan of women drivin' up the Alaska Highway, I thought it would be a chance to do some serious paintin', and besides, Alaska sounded like about as far away as I could get from Riley's Holler and still be in the U.S. of A.

The women on this trip is good people and they understand why I paint. When I describe the light, they tell me they can see it, too. That is just so nice, because people back home can't see the sense of me "wastin' my time" paintin'." But, I know I ain't crazy. See, one of my goals is to own a art gallery. Time's 'a runnin' out on that one, 'cuz I turned 28 this year and it isn't goin' to happen if I stay in Arkansas. It'll be on a farm for orphan cats, so Lucy and Ethel can grow old with lots of friends around 'em.

Like I was sayin', the light in Alaska is incredible. It's intense and it's always changin'. During twilight, which lasts nearly all night this time of year, it is glorious to behold. The sky turns a reddish-pink, with layers of purple and orange, and it never quite gets dark. While the others are sleepin', I'm out there paintin', capturin' it on canvas.

I started paintin' when I was a child. Momma once told me, may she rest in peace, that I used to fingerpaint with my food when I was little and she didn't stop me, 'cuz she loved to watch what I done with the colors. When I was growin' up, it was the Great Depression and money was real hard to come by, but Momma got herself ahold of a second-hand camera, so she could take pictures of my "paintin's." That was a wonderful thing she done.

I started to paint a lot when I was 17, the year I had my baby. See, what happened was this. Our school principal come to my class to judge some paintin's we done for an open house display. He starts talkin' to me and says my paintin's are real good and that I have a lot of talent. Now, nobody had ever told me they liked my paintin's before, 'cept Momma, of course, and he was just so charmin'. So, he offers to drive me home – he says it's no problem, it's on his way. When we get to the house, Momma isn't there and he asks if he can come in for a drink of water. I didn't see no harm – it was real hot outside. I turned my back to get him a glass of water and the next thing I know, he's on me like a tick on a hound.

I had to quit school when I started showin'. I had the baby at home – it was a little girl – Momma took a picture of her and then the woman from the Family Service come and took her away. I didn't have a chance to name her, but I still have the photograph. After they took her away, is when I started dreamin' about the light and paintin' like crazy. A few months later, I found Lucy and Ethel.

Lately, I've been dreamin' about children and I've been paintin' pictures of little girls. They're always surrounded by light, and they're always smilin'. Sometimes, I wonder where my little girl is and what she's doin', and I just pray she's happy and livin' in the light.

Lights Fade

The End

AIN'T I A WOMAN
by Nicole Goodwin

ABOUT THE PLAY

A poem.

Ain't I A Woman

I never knew what it meant
To be a woman.

I treated my womanhood like an
Old pair of jeans.

Ready to wear, and then
Throw in the hamper when need be.

It wasn't until my friend became sick,
That my eyes were opened.

You see the chemo took her hair away,
Made it retreat from her scalp in clumps.

Her hair for me was her signature thing.
Those long brown locks, were now gone.

Nowhere to be found.
No point of return,
She decided to go bald.

I decided to tag along.

Her husband cut off my hair,
And took what was left of hers.
His shiny clippers scalped us to the roots.

145

Leaving nothing to the imagination.
And as the breeze of winter blew
Over my head,

I realized that she and I were women.
And nothing can ever remove that truth.

No cancer, not baldness.
Not death or fear of the unknown.

The End

SISTER
by Mercedes Sanchez

ABOUT THE PLAY
A Monologue

Character:
Paula – 60, female

Sister

PAULA
(Woman – 60 years old)

My sister, Mary, had the best laugh in the world...it was a real belly laugh and it sounded so joyful. She was smart too. Mary was the first person in our family to go to college. She wanted to be a nurse. Father grumbled that he was wasting his money educating a girl, she would probably just get married anyway but at least she would find a quality husband at that college.

Mary and I would stay up late talking and laughing. My favorite thing was falling asleep to the sound of her laughter. We talked all the time...mostly about our future, boys, and complaining how strict our parents were. We weren't allowed to go anywhere but school and church. When we asked Father why he was so strict, he would mumble that his daughters were nice girls and boys only had one thing on their minds. When we got older and learned about where babies come from, we discovered one of our family secrets. Mary was a "miracle baby." She was allegedly 2 months premature...and weighed a healthy 7 ½ pounds. We laughed ourselves silly when we realized Father had been one of those boys with only one thing on his mind. That knowledge didn't stay humorous...it later became just another lie.

I missed Mary when she went away to college. She would write to me all the time and call when she could. She flourished at school and said she couldn't wait for me to join her there. Mary fell in love with a boy named Michael. She confided, with her special laugh, that she understood why boys only had one thing on their minds. She called me a few months later crying that she was in trouble, pregnant. She didn't want to get married, she wanted to finish school. She said Michael found a real doctor that could take care of it.

Mary died 43 years ago – a few days before the Roe v Wade decision. It was the middle of the night when my parents got the call. Mary had died of some kind of infection...they didn't explain and I didn't tell them I knew what had really happened. I cried for days, hiding out in our room until the funeral. It was at the burial that I heard the lie for the first time. They said my sister had died in a car accident while away at college. I couldn't get out of my head that my beautiful sister's birth was a lie and so was her death. It seemed so wrong and disrespectful. When everyone had left and we were alone at her grave, I couldn't hold it in. "I know Mary didn't die in a car accident. Why did you have to lie?" Mother started to cry. Father calmly said, "You are not going to college." I left home after that. I worked my way through college on my own. Eventually, I did reconcile with my parents. We never talk about Mary's death. We hide behind our happy memories her.

People always ask me how I feel about the attacks on women's rights. You can quote me, "It's bullshit and it makes me fucking angry." We can't lose the rights we gained...we can't lose any more women and girls. It's literally a matter of life and death. I became a nurse, like Mary wanted to be, and I worked at an abortion clinic for many years. I saw my sister in all the girls we helped. I loved my job. Sometimes it was hard work...emotionally draining. But after every hard day, as I started to fall asleep...I swear I could hear her laugh...my sister's proud, joyful laugh.

The End

SPARE RIB (excerpts)
by Winter Miller

ABOUT THE PLAY

Two monologues; excerpts from the full-length play, *Spare Rib*.
(To engage with the full-length play Spare Rib, from which these two monologues are excerpted, please contact the author through her website, www.wintermiller.com)

Spare Rib

FETUS 2:

I want the rights of personhood.
I want to drive the car. To be obligated to wear a seatbelt. I want to obey the speed
limit or if not, get arrested.

I want to go out and join the military.
I need to vote.
I need to buy beer for my friends. I need to buy beer to be popular.
I want to own property.
I want life support.
I want to use birth control whenever I want.
I want First Amendment rights all the time.
I want to wear shorts when it's 20 below. I want to avoid baldness of any sort.
I need health insurance.
I want to get my nose done so it's bigger.
I need a lot of friends with benefits.
I need to get paid. I need a tax refund.
I want to bear arms. I want to arm bears.
Whatever I want, I want.
Whatever I need, I get.
My freedom.
I need you to consider the child's "best interest" only when it matches what I am interested in.
I want to speak freely but I want you to shut the fuck up when you don't say what I want you to say.
I have rights. My rights are God-given. Everything I do is my right.
It's my right not to leave this womb.
I can stay here as long as I want: Eminent Domain.
Also: This is my home: Possession is 9/10ths of the law.
I need a longer gestation. I don't know how long. Months, years... we'll see. I'll see.
I need to decide for myself. I am certainly not causing anyone else any harm.
Sheeeee can suck it, I have rights.
I also want to order a pizza. I need to get a job. I need to buy a car.
I will follow the law or if I don't I need to be punished.
I have the right to a vaccine or to refuse the vaccine.
I'm not coming out of here.
I don't trust that as soon as I leave here my rights will ever be as important again.
I have a right to life. I am going to exercise that here in this womb.

I don't even like gravity.
I have the right not to chew my food.
Four pounds is my goal weight.
If anybody cuts her open and takes me out you are violating my rights.
In my home, my rules.

FETUS 3:

I am hands, feet, everything new. We have secrets that are passed here. The way trees have rings inside to mark their age. I know there were others who passed before me. Three, precisely. The oldest lives on the outside. The second was scooped out and placed in a plastic jar with others and others. I await my fate. I do not care, either way, whether I go to the jar or whether I go to the outside.
I know I return again and again because I have already lived, already returned, already lived, already returned, I am different each time.
I was an ant. That didn't last very long.
I was an elk, which was possibly my favorite so far.
I was a yellow marigold, which was also very brief.
I was a grape, a seedless, red.
I was, again briefly, a moth. I didn't love moth-hood, it was somewhat treacherous.
Though it was great to really be obsessed with a light bulb... gave me purpose.
I was a Dutch Elm for years.
I was a marmoset, but that was quick due to an accident.
I was a termite, that seemed to last forever. Really boring, but I liked having the one
thing to focus on.
I was that.
Right now I'm this.
Later I will be something else.
Maybe a bunny.
Maybe a crocus.
Those two are on my wish list, but it's always changing.

End of excerpts

SECTION: CLOSING
Directed by Stacey Linnartz

BLESSED
by Alix Olson

ABOUT THE PLAY

A spoken word piece, this is excerpted from a longer selection. The work was performed at the Reproductive Freedom Festival by three actors, who sometimes deliver lines in choral fashion.

blessed

she was blessed with a family that threw her up high, said flap your brains girl it's time we test drive the sky and she did not know where she was headed, but it had to be more than what she was leaving behind so she grabbed her life by the scruff of its years she let loose the reigns and she went for a ride and it helped that she was friendly cause she'd smile when she'd say what she'd say so she felt armed to be a hero, the impossible kind with the big dagger flaw and the world loomed like a tragedy, she'd never seen one up so close before there was daunting poverty, and there was haunting wealth and the narrator warned her to keep to herself the people were petty. and precious, their faces were preserved in stone and the chorus insisted she leave them alone. so, she peeked behind the curtain at the mainstream stage everything there was colorful and strange, cellphones patrolled the streets connecting fools from brain to brain and she put one hand on her head and other on her heart and she swore to all she knew that she would never be able to tell them apart and she says, i guess that i am prey to all these things that i condemn and i confess perhaps that's why i am as pissed off as i am. so i'll keep one hand on my head and the other on my heart and i'll swear to all i know

151

that i will never be able to tell them apart. and yeah, she is just one citizen with her hands tied behind her back and this is why she chooses to use her teeth and tongue to attack. this is why you gotta use your mouth to fight back. cause you got one hand on your head and the other on your heart, and you're swearing to all you know that you will never be able to tell them apart. you're swearing to all you know that they will never be able to tear them apart. but we are blessed with this family, that has thrown us up and i say flap your brains, it's time we test drive the sky and we may not know where we are headed, but it has got to be more than what we're leaving behind so let's grab our lives by the scruff of their years, let's let loose the reins and let's go for this ride. let's go for this ride.

The End

SECTION SEVEN, SPECIAL SECTION: IRELAND 2016
Originally directed by Thais Flaitt Giannoccaro

Savita by Samantha Lierens
The Renunciation by the home|work Collective

SAVITA
by Samantha Lierens

ABOUT THE PLAY

Characters
Savita: 17 weeks pregnant, young Indian woman.
Parveen: Savita's husband, 34 yr old Indian engineer.
Midwife: 50 ish, white Irish woman.
Nurse: 20-something woman.
Consultant: Attractive, professional 30s. Man or woman.

Savita

Scene 1

Savita and Parveen in Background. Midwife and Nurse at front.

MIDWIFE
(reading notes)
Savita Halappanavar. 31 years old, presented Saturday evening. She's 17 weeks along and miscarrying: cervix is fully dilated. She's a dentist, an Indian National, she's lived in Ireland four years. She's here with her husband, Parveen.

153

NURSE
Halappanavar? That's a mouthful.

MIDWIFE
...She's in a great deal of pain.

NURSE
It's never a walk in the park.

Nurse goes back to Savita. Parveen comes forwards to midwife.

PARVEEN
Please. It's been a day and a half now and nothing seems to be happening.

MIDWIFE
It's a horrible experience to go through, Mr. Halappanavar. We're making your wife as comfortable as we can.

And how about you? Have you gone down to our canteen at all?

In background, nurse pats Savita's shoulder, leaves.

PARVEEN
I thought it was back pain at first. We were watching X-factor and she said it hurt but she wasn't too worried.

MIDWIFE
I'm so very sorry.

PARVEEN
We just want to go home. My wife is helping to organize the Dilwali festival. It's only a few weeks away.

MIDWIFE
That sounds like something positive for you both to look forward to.

PARVEEN
Do you know Divali?

MIDWIFE
Not really...

PARVEEN
It's the festival of lights. A celebration. There will be lots of singing, dancing, good food. Savita loves it. She is supposed to be hosting a meeting about it at our house. She doesn't want to let anyone down.

MIDWIFE
I'm sure everyone will understand.

PARVEEN
She still thinks we might be home in time.

MIDWIFE
It can take some time to recover...emotionally as well as physically.

PARVEEN
Savita loves to be organized. She plans everything. Price comparisons. Cots, pushchairs, nappies. We were even arguing about names...

MIDWIFE
Mr. Halappanavar, your wife is young and strong. God willing, there will be other babies.

PARVEEN
We wanted this one.

Savita screams. Midwife and Parveen dash back to her.

SAVITA
Please hurry it up. I can't endure this much longer.

MIDWIFE
Your waters have broken, my dear. It won't be long now.

SAVITA
They said that yesterday. Please. I want an induction, a termination. Anything.

MIDWIFE
It's happening, Savita, it is. All the signs are here.

Savita cries out.

SAVITA
It hurts so much. Isn't there a pessary? A tablet I can take?

MIDWIFE
I'll talk to someone.

PARVEEN
They are all saying the same to us: We have to wait it out.

MIDWIFE
I'll see what I can do.

Consultant and Midwife at front. Parveen and Savita remain.

CONSULTANT
But there's still a fetal heartbeat?

MIDWIFE
Yes but...this has been going on for (checks watch) fifty-six hours now. She is pleading for medical management.

CONSULTANT
Poor fetal progress does not provide legal grounds for termination, as you know. Let it run its course.

MIDWIFE
We could do something.

CONSULTANT
Like what?

MIDWIFE
The Supreme Court ruled that we could carry out an abortion if a woman's life is at risk from the continued pregnancy.

CONSULTANT
Well...is there a real and substantial risk to the life of the mother here?

MIDWIFE
I don't know.

CONSULTANT
Not merely the *health* of the mother, AnnMarie, her life has to be at real and substantial risk.

MIDWIFE
By the time her life is at risk it may be too late.

CONSULTANT
These are the cards we have been dealt with. We are constrained by the constitution. As it stands there is no legal certainty as to when we can intervene.

Don't look at me like that. In fifteen years, we have not had one maternal mortality in this hospital, not one...

MIDWIFE
Perhaps one of the reasons our statistics are so good, is that the women with complications travel to England...

CONSULTANT
...And we are not going to have one now.

MIDWIFE
...Eleven pregnant women leave Ireland every single day.

PARVEEN
(from back of stage, shouting)
Will someone please help her?

CONSULTANT
Unfortunately then, it appears that Savita and her husband chose to live in the wrong country. We can't carry out their request here.

MIDWIFE
The fetus is ... non-viable. It hasn't been since she arrived on Saturday. Since before that, probably.

CONSULTANT
Ann-Marie, terminating a live fetus is illegal. We could be subject to a criminal prosecution and imprisoned.

Savita cries out.

MIDWIFE
This is a farce.

CONSULTANT
I am protecting you, my team and the entirety of The Galway hospital.
Try and make her comfortable. Has her husband been to the canteen?

MIDWIFE
I guess.

CONSULTANT
As long as that fetus has a heartbeat, our hands are tied. Do you understand?

MIDWIFE
She is fully dilated. She is a gaping wound, a sitting duck for an infection.

CONSULTANT
And there is a gaping hole in our law. And I am not prepared to breach it.

Consultant leaves. Midwife tries to calm down/slow breathing. She goes back to see Savita and Parveen. They look up, hopeful.

MIDWIFE
The Consultant is just...finishing her rounds.

PARVEEN
We are begging for your help, please.

MIDWIFE
It's not that simple.

PARVEEN
I understand...How much do you need? How much do we have to pay?

MIDWIFE
Put your wallet away.

PARVEEN
Then what? My wife is a dentist. A professional.

SAVITA
I try to help people. Every day. I do my best.

PARVEEN
She is a hard-working woman. We have never had hand-outs here.

SAVITA
(weeping)
Fillings, removal of wisdom teeth, abscess, I do it all.
(pause)
This is too slow. It's dangerous. I know what is happening.

PARVEEN
You said the baby won't make it. But my wife? She is here and now.

SAVITA
We want three children. We are turning the box room into a nursery. I hand-made the curtains. Peter Rabbit.

PARVEEN
Why won't you do something?

MIDWIFE
We just can't.

PARVEEN
Why not?

MIDWIFE
Because...because this is a Catholic Country.

HUSBAND
But we are not Catholics!!

SAVITA
I am a Hindu. Please. We have different Gods you and me.
My Gods will understand. Explain it to her, Parveen. Per-
haps she thinks we are terrorists?

Midwife and Parveen move to the front.

PARVEEN
You can't imagine our excitement when the visas were
approved. You can't imagine. All our hard work, all our
dreams. We left India for a better life. We wanted to have
our family in a place of progress, a place with a future.

MIDWIFE
Yes. But this is Ireland.

PARVEEN
Exactly. This is 21st century Europe.
She is in terrible pain. Why won't you help her?

Savita crawls on the floor. Parveen wrings his hands.

PARVEEN (cont'd)
This is not a third world country.

SAVITA
Help me – or I will take it out with my own hands.

Consultant arrives

CONSULTANT (authoritatively)
I thought your shift had finished, Nurse?
Go home. Get some rest. Savita is in safe hands.

Midwife hesitantly leaves.

CONSULTANT (cont'd)
Now, Parveen. Why don't you go down and get some tea while I see to your wife?

They take everything away.

End of Scene

Scene 2

Parveen and Savita and mattress and chair are no longer there.
Midwife comes back, coat and handbag, all smiles.

NURSE
Perfect Autumn day, isn't it? I got you an iced bun. I know you like them.

MIDWIFE (eats)
Mm, thank you. So. How's Savita doing?

NURSE
Savita?

MIDWIFE
Halappanavar.

NURSE
Oh Hala what a palavar. The fetus still had a heartbeat right up until Wednesday morning. They had everyone in

there. The situation was explained to them hundreds of times. Made no difference: they keep begging for a...you know what. Raging he was. 'It is her right'. I've never heard anything like it.

(pause)

Then...she collapsed in the toilet, Wednesday night. E-Coli infection.
She's in ICU now.

MIDWIFE
What?

NURSE
I know it's tough, Ann Marie, but it's the best place for her.

MIDWIFE (shocked)
Wh-y?

NURSE
They're talking septicemia. Possible organ failure.

Parveen walks by, disheveled. Midwife puts her hand on his arm.

PARVEEN
Ah, it's you, Doctor...

MIDWIFE
I'm... not...

PARVEEN
...I wanted to tell you I cancelled in the end.

MIDWIFE
Sorry?

PARVEEN
The Divali meeting. She didn't want me to, but I did.

MIDWIFE
Oh? Yes. I remember.

PARVEEN
Savita loves to dance. When we're at a party, she makes me dance on the stage with her. I used to hate going on the stage but I promised, for her, I will do anything.

End of Scene 2

End of Play

THE RENUNCIATION
by The home|work Collective

ABOUT THE PLAY

Performed by three performers at the Reproductive Freedom Festival, this version of the text is 'The Renunciation as performed for The Reproductive Freedom Festival.' For the original text, go to www.homeworkcollective.tumblr. com.

'The Renunciation' is a performed reading that intervenes, respectfully, in the reflective space offered by the modern day Angelus. This work contains stories that describe a set of social rituals for 12+ people from Ireland seeking abortions daily. Read aloud, the verses publicly present uncensored

164

insights into lived experiences. Both rhythm and structure reference the Hail Mary prayer that commemorates the moment in which Mary exercised her agency in consenting to becoming pregnant. The verses are intended to highlight the detrimental consequences of denying that same agency for others and disregarding our consent - in essence, attempting to enforce pregnancy on us. 'The Renunciation' challenges the double standards dictated by idealized notions of womanhood and mothering that overlook present day realities and less-than-ideal circumstances.

'The Renunciation' is a production by home | work, a group title that refers to the domestic policies of the Irish state that preclude access to abortion in Ireland. It is also a nod to the traditional sphere of work of women on the island and the practice of making change from within. The home | work collectively confronts the themes of censorship and self-censorship through art, action, performance, conversation and camaraderie. *(Editor's Note: After extensive advocacy, abortion laws in Ireland were finally liberalized in December 2018.)*

The Renunciation

Opening

PERFORMER
The government decreed unto the people of Ireland

ALL
Thus 12 women are exiled everyday

Verse 1

PERFORMER
At 27, she does not want to be a mother. She lives with her boyfriend and they agree.

ALL
She has overcome obstacles to abortion before and ten years later she faces the same ones again. A Woman.

PERFORMER
People of Ireland, raise your voices

ALL
We are all worthy of our right to choose

Verse 2

PERFORMER
He is transgender and spent 3 hours at Dublin Airport to make them understand why his passport states he is female.

ALL
The contraception failed once and he had to explain his life to a stranger. A Man.

PERFORMER
People of Ireland, raise your voices

ALL
We are all worthy of our right to choose

Verse 3

PERFORMER
She had 15 Summers to her name. She was raped and is pregnant. Her parents brought her to England for an abortion.

ALL
She lied to school and friends, afraid of their judgment. She said she was going to England for a holiday. A Girl.

PERFORMER
People of Ireland, raise your voices

ALL
We are all worthy of our right to choose

Verse 4

PERFORMER
He minded their kids while she travelled with a heavy heart after the diagnosis of fatal fetal abnormality.

ALL
Speaking a foreign tongue, they faced the sorrow alone, one away and the other at home. A Man.

PERFORMER
People of Ireland, raise your voices

ALL
We are all worthy of our right to choose

Verse 5

PERFORMER
She was a student studying to improve her chances in life, saving for fees, when they made a mistake.

ALL
Because of one mistake now half of her fee will cover the aeroplane ticket. A Woman.

PERFORMER
People of Ireland, raise your voices

ALL
We are all worthy of our right to choose

Verse 6

PERFORMER
She is 23 and had a baby. They are both living with HIV.
She is a recovering addict. Every day is a struggle.

ALL
She knows she can't afford another baby. She can't even
afford this. She borrows money to travel. A Woman.

PERFORMER
People of Ireland, raise your voices

ALL
We are all worthy of our right to choose

Verse 7

PERFORMER
She had to travel all the way to London from Northern
Ireland: a second class citizen despite her UK passport

ALL
Even though she paid her taxes just the same, she was not
afforded cover by the NHS as others are. A Woman.

PERFORMER
People of Ireland, raise your voices

ALL
We are all worthy of our right to choose

Verse 8

PERFORMER
She was an asylum seeker, arrived pregnant after being raped. She tried to get to England but was sent back by the powers that be.

ALL
She found help online, ordered abortion pills and had them delivered to her from the North. A Woman.

PERFORMER
People of Ireland, raise your voices

ALL
We are all worthy of our right to choose

Verse 9

PERFORMER
She had a previous child with severe disabilities. She cares for him every hour of the day and night.

ALL
Another child would mean less care for her first. She can't. She travels to England. A Woman.

PERFORMER
People of Ireland, raise your voices

ALL
We are all worthy of our right to choose

Verse 10

PERFORMER
While her cancer was in remission, she got pregnant and it endangered her chance of recovery.

ALL
A passport out of date delayed her journey more. She never recovered after that. A Woman.

PERFORMER
People of Ireland, raise your voices

ALL
We are all worthy of our right to choose

Verse 11

PERFORMER
She was against the idea of abortion until she needed one herself. She told a friend who supported her choice.

ALL
They travelled to England together. She told everyone they were going shopping. A Woman.

PERFORMER
People of Ireland, raise your voices

ALL
We are all worthy of our right to choose

Verse 12

PERFORMER
She needed an abortion but had no money to travel and no time to smuggle pills from the North.

ALL
She found a cheap backstreet abortion but it has cost her health and fertility ever since. A Woman.

PERFORMER
People of Ireland, raise your voices

ALL
We are all worthy of our right to choose

Closing

PERFORMER
The government decreed unto the people of Ireland

ALL
Thus 12 women are exiled everyday

PERFORMER
The amendment was made law

ALL
And we live as criminals

PERFORMER
People of Ireland, raise your voices

ALL
We are all worthy of our right to choose
We are all worthy of our right to choose
We are all worthy of our right to choose

The End

SECTION EIGHT, SPECIAL SECTION: TWO SONGS

Not So Fresh Feeling by Marjorie Duffield, Greg Pliska
These Breasts Can Kill by Marjorie Duffield, Greg Pliska

NOT SO FRESH FEELING and THESE BREASTS CAN KILL
by Marjorie Duffield

ABOUT THE PLAY

Not So Fresh Feeling and **These Breasts Can Kill** are song lyrics developed as part of "Tit Tales" - A Body-Politics Cabaret (book and lyrics by Marjorie Duffield, music by Greg Pliska).

Not So Fresh Feelin'
(Song lyrics)

JILL
I've got that not so fresh feelin'
Creepin' up on me
'Cause a woman can have odors
And special cleansing needs

SABRINA
When you're feelin'
Down and dirty and you need a little boost

KELLY
Something delicately fragranced
Don't use ordinary douche

SABRINA/KELLY
You gotta give her
Fresh country flowers
Cool mountain breeze
Spring rain freshness
Pine forest trees

KELLY
Cleaner, fresher, more refreshing

JILL
I want confidence that lasts

SABRINA
Skip the vinegar and water

KELLY
And the baking soda's past

ALL
You gotta give her
Fresh cuntry flowers
Cool mountain breeze
Spring rain freshness
Pine forest trees

JILL
'Cause a woman can have odors
And she needs a little boost
Something delicately fragranced
Don't use ordinary douche

SABRINA/KELLY
Fresh country flowers

The End

These Breasts Can Kill
(Song lyrics)

(We hear the clip clop of Hope's heals. Then a whistle. Two "men" accost her.)

ACTOR #2
Hey, Baby.

ACTOR #1
Are those real?

ACTOR #2
Like to get me some of those.

ACTOR #1
Ooh, Mama.

ACTOR #2
Hey, baby.

ACTOR #1
Cute cantaloupes.

ACTOR #2
Great grapefruits.

ACTOR #1
Terrific tomatoes.

ACTOR #2
Come on, baby.

HOPE
Please leave me alone.

ACTOR #1
Lighten up little girl.

ACTOR #2
You know you love it.

HOPE
I need to get by.

ACTOR #1
You have no sense of humor.

ACTOR #2
Take it easy sweetheart.

ACTOR #1
It was just a joke.

ACTOR #2
A joke.

ACTOR #1
But check out those Hooters.

ACTOR #2
Kajoobies.

ACTOR #1
Melons.

ACTOR #2
Bazoombas.

ACTOR #1
Major Globes.

ACTOR #2
Rack action.

HOPE
(Trying to pass.)
I really have to go.

ACTOR #1
Want to give me a ride on those Winnebagos?

ACTOR #2
Better turn on those headlights.

(Hope is surrounded. There is no way out. She softens, and plays their game with Betty-Boop innocence.)

HOPE
I love it when you call them names
And give them your attention
It makes me feel all warm inside
With every word you mention

I love it when you call them names
And though we've never met
You seem to think you have the right
Comes with your dick I guess

I love it when you call them names
But there's one thing iIshould tell you
Your life's is over, get out now
I've no control, I'm danger!

These breasts can kill
They've killed before
They pack a gun
They'll shoot you down

ACTORS 1 & 2
To the floor

HOPE
Or suffocate
'Til there's no air

ACTORS 1 & 2
Titties, torpedoes, headlights, bazooms
Watermelons, grapefruits, cantaloupes, balloons
Hooters, shooters, tooters, tomatoes
Bazongas, bazoombies and Winnebegos

HOPE
You want to make me feel ashamed
While smiling at your comments
You hope that I will hurry by
And scurry off in silence

But I love it when you call them names
And there's one thing I should tell you
Your life's is over, get out now
I've no control, I'm danger!

These breasts can kill
They've killed before
They pack a gun
They'll shoot you down

ACTORS 1 & 2
To the floor

HOPE
Or suffocate
'Til there's no air
You're gasping hard
And begging please

ACTORS 1 & 2
Please no more

HOPE
And with their teeth
They'll spot you out
Or take a bit
Then eat you up

ACTORS 1 & 2
These breasts can kill
I know they will
Won't stop until you're dead

ALL
Won't stop until bang, bang your dead!

At the end of the song, HOPE 'shoots' ACTOR 1 & 2 with her breasts.

HOPE
Getta load of THOSE Bazooms!

The End

SECTION NINE, SPECIAL SECTION:
Additional Writings
Tru Luv by Cindy Cooper
Why I March by Zoneziwoh Mbondgulo-Wondieh

TRU LUV
by Cindy Cooper

ABOUT THE PLAY

A short play from the Words of Choice collection that toured to 20 states.

Tru Luv

Characters:
MOM: A progressive Mom.
DAD: A liberal Dad
MARLA: An enlightened teen, the daughter of MOM and DAD

The setting is a contemporary American home, a cozy modern place with a progressive mom, MOM, and a liberal dad, DAD, and an enlightened teen, MARLA, all cohabiting comfortably in mutual happiness and deep regard for one another. Life is wonderful. MOM and DAD are sitting in the living room when MARLA enters.

MARLA
(Enters.)
Mom, Dad ...

DAD
What is it, honey?

MARLA
I've got something I want to say. It's a little scary. I'm afraid after I tell you, you won't love me anymore.

MOM
You can tell us anything, dear.

DAD
Absolutely, toostie pop.

MARLA
Well, I'm in love.

DAD
That's wonderful.

MOM
Anyone we know?

MARLA
No.

DAD
Then tell us who it is ....

MARLA
I don't know if I can.

MOM
Oh, sweetie, are you worried it's someone we won't like?

MARLA
It's hard to tell.

DAD
If you're worried that it's someone of another race or religion or background, that's really ok with us, as long as you are happy. Is it someone you met at school?

MARLA
No.

MOM
We accept all people into our lives. A same-sex relationship is alright with us. Is it someone that works at the hospital where you are volunteering?

MARLA
Kind of. Ok. Here goes. Lately, at the hospital, I've been helping in the lab area – filling orders, tracking samples ...

MOM
Yes, so you've said.

MARLA
Mom, dad: I fell in love with a stem cell.
Pulls out a container.
Look.

DAD
But ...

MOM
It's so ... little ...

MARLA
You think just because it's little, it isn't alive. You think because it's a stem cell, it doesn't have feelings and concerns.

DAD
Looking at container.
I can't actually see anything.

MOM
To Dad.
It's that little dot ... there ... like a piece of pepper. Or salt.

MARLA
It's so-o cute! I can't wait for it to be implanted in a womb and become a zygote and then some day an embryo and then a fetus. And when it's finally born, we can go off together ...

MOM
Honey, wouldn't that be robbing the cradle.

MARLA
Grabs the container back.
I <u>knew</u> you wouldn't understand. We're leaving!
SHE drops the container.
Oh no! My stem cell! My love!
SHE sobs.

DAD
Honey, don't worry, there's more than one fish in the sea.

MARLA
I'll never find another stem cell like that. Never! Never never. I was in love with a stem cell and now that stem cell is gone. My life is over!
SHE exits.

MOM and DAD
Looking on the floor, swapping lines, quickly and overlapping.
(D) Maybe we can find it.
(M) It's got to be here somewhere.
(D) It wasn't bad-looking, if you could see it.
(M) I never said it was bad-looking.
(D) Oh the truth is, we've failed as parents!
They hug.

MOM
We'll keep trying. We'll get it right, darling, we will.

The End

WHY I MARCH
by Zoneziwoh Mbondgulo-Wondieh

ABOUT THE PLAY

A poem and anthem written performed in Reproductive Freedom Is What We Want, a radio drama presented by Words of Choice in spring 2017.

Why I March

I march for myself. I march for my safety. I march to be a voice for change.
I march for the millions of women and girls who live under the worst forms of dictatorship and tyranny.
I march for those who are unable to freely exercise their constitutional and democratic rights to freedom of expression and choice.
I march because I am tired of hearing officials make promises in meetings and at events, only to see very little action taken to bring these promises to fruition.
I march because it is time to let everyone know that the world is failing at advancing women's rights.
I march for the millions of women and human rights defenders who receive death threats, who are sentenced to jail, and who are killed for challenging dictatorial regimes and speaking up against injustice.
I march because, at the moment, my government is legalizing and normalizing State-sponsored violence, policing of women's bodies, and the imprisonment of those who speak truth to power.

I march because it is my human and democratic right to march.

The End

USING PLAYS OR SELECTIONS FROM THIS PUBLICATION

Use of Plays
All of the works in this volume are subject to the copyright of the author. This means that the plays may only be performed with specific permission of the writer. The best approach is to contact the writer listed in the section called WRITERS at the beginning of this collection. Contact the writer before you make plans to perform the selection: most are eager to help. If you are unable to reach the writer, you can reach out to reproductivefreedomfestival@gmail.com with the subject heading: Permission.

More Information

For additional information, including resources on reproductive freedom and rights, activist steps and a listening packet, visit the **Reproductive Freedom Festival** website, **www.reproductivefreedomfestival.org.**

Short Plays on Reproductive Freedom is a publication of *Words of Choice, Inc.* Information about Words of Choice is available at **www.wordsofchoice.org.**

Contact Us:
reproductivefreedomfestival@gmail.com

Notes

Notes

www.ingramcontent.com/pod-product-compliance
Lightning Source LLC
Chambersburg PA
CBHW060506290526
45791CB00001B/285